BRIGID BISHOP

Tarot Journal

BRIGID BISHOP PRESENTS:

Tarot Journal

ISBN-13: 978-1475109740
ISBN-10: 1475109741

Freeland, PA 18224 USA
www.brigidbishop.com

Dedication

This book is dedicated to my mother in loving memory of her sweet soul. I miss you every day mom.

Brigid Bishop

Other Books by Brigid Bishop

Uncloaking the Tarot, November 2011

Uncloaking the Tarot Workbook Companion and Tarot Journal, October 2012

The Dating Game: Insights into Affairs of The Heart, April 2010

Brigid Bishop's Little Book of Magick Spells, Releasing Summer 2012

Tarot Journals Volumes 1 Through 24, March 2012

Introduction

What the Tarot Is, What the Tarot is Not

What the Tarot is, is a tool for stimulating personal spiritual growth. The Tarot, known by the general public as primarily a divinatory tool, has much more productive uses than divination for the enlightened and educated individual.

What the Tarot is not, is a fortune telling mechanism that will predict exactly what the course of events of your life will be. Although the Tarot can be used effectively for divination, the Tarot will only present to the Reader what will happen if the current course of events remains unaltered, so Free Will always allows you to alter the future presented in the cards, either in a positive or adverse manner. It is key for the Reader and the Querent to mark specifically what path they are on consciously in order for a Reading to be an effective consultation of the esoteric.

Myths and Misconceptions

Myths and misconceptions concerning the Tarot abound. One popular myth is that you should never read your own cards. Let me dispel that for you right now with one logical statement: The Tarot is meant to be a meditational tool, assisting us with the introspection process, if we are not to read our own cards, then how will they be an effective tool for our own personal spiritual growth.

Although there is danger that we will project our hopes and fears onto the spread when we read our own cards, this can be avoided if prior to reading we focus on our question and meditate on the statement "not my hopes, not my fears, but the truth". Maintaining this meditational sentence in our consciousness while working with the cards will assist us in eliminating any corruption of a personal self-reading.

Another misconception is that the Tarot has something to do with the practice of some dark, magickal, or evil force. Call it what you will. Quite to the contrary, the Tarot is a holy and mystical part of understanding what our souls were meant to do on this earthly plane, what lessons we were put here to learn, and how to better serve the human race. Understanding with others begins with understanding ourselves. How can we interact effectively with the rest of the human race if we lack the basic understanding of the psychological and emotional motives that drive us to behave in the manners that we do. The Tree of Life, as presented by the Holy Qabalah, is an ancient and spiritual path to wholeness of the soul, there is nothing evil about it. The Tarot brings us closer to the God and Goddess within, and helps us to live among the various states of evolution our sisters and brothers on this earthly plane exist in, in peace and harmony.

The Tarot Deck

The Tarot Deck consists of 78 cards. 22 of these cards are referred to as the "Major Arcana" and the remaining 56 are known as the "Minor Arcana".

The *Major Arcana* are the most powerful cards in the deck. The twenty-two archetypical members represent archetypes of the human soul's journey through development. Each member has powerful spiritual and divinatory implications; we will review each card individually, in order to expedite a comprehensive understanding of the deck.

The Major Arcana are drenched in symbolism and relate to not only reincarnation, internal development, external forces, numerology and astrology, but tie in to nearly every esoteric principle that exists.

When a member of the Major Arcana appears in a spread, it represents forces that are beyond the Querent's control. They tend to represent either the actions of others who have influence over the situation, or the role of fate, karma, destiny, or whatever you prefer to refer to it as.

The important thing to remember when working with the cards is that we must learn to accept the things that are beyond our control, and focus on those things which we can control (ourselves). Remember this: Never let something that is out of your control upset you, the only factor we can control in this life is ourselves. If we come to a challenging situation in life, reflect upon what factors you could and could not control, and adjust your behaviors accordingly. With this in mind, the Tarot can help you look inward for guidance.

The *Minor Arcana* consists of "court" cards and the "pip" cards in four suits. The court cards are the Page, Knight, Queen, and King, the pip cards consist of the ace through ten. If you noticed that this almost sounds like the structure of a modern deck of playing cards, you are on track with the course of study already. The modern deck arose from the Tarot, the Page has been eliminated, and the balance of the deck remains intact. The Knight is commonly referred to as the Jack, and the four suits of the Tarot are commonly called: Wands, Cups, Swords, and Pentacles, replaced respectively with Clubs, Hearts, Spades, and Diamonds.

Tarot Decks sometimes vary the names of the suits, common alternate names are as follows; Pentacles, also referred to as "Coins", "Shields" or "Disks". Wands are sometimes called "Rods", "Staffs" or "Spears". Cups may sometimes be referred to as "Hearts", "Horns" or "Waterskins". Swords in some decks are referred to as "Daggers". The decks of different cultures may have various alternate suit names, but the meanings remain the same, regardless of what we refer to the suit as.

The Suit of Wands refers to action being taken. It is associated with the Element of Fire, the South Quarter of the Circle, the Season of Spring, and the time of day of Noon. Typically, a Wand appearing in a spread will indicate movement or action of some kind. The Qabalah assigns the Letter I from the ancient Hebraic Alphabet to it. Astrologically, the signs of Aries, Leo and Sagittarius are represented by the Wands.

The Suit of Cups is associated with emotion, love and human relationships, when predominant in a spread it nearly always pertains to matters of the heart. The Season of Summer, the West Quarter of the Circle, the Element of Water, the Letter O and Dusk are associated with Cups. The corresponding Astrological signs arc Pisces, Cancer and Scorpio.

The Swords are representative of the Autumn, of things perhaps coming to an end. Many of the pip cards in the Swords Suit are associated with pain, or painful forced change, but not all. Swords represent the East Quarter of the Circle, the Element of Air, the Letter E, and Dawn. Swords represent the intellectual in many cases. The Astrological signs of Aquarius, Gemini and Libra are reflected in this Suit.

The fourth Suit, Pentacles, represents all that is material, and successes on the earthly plane. Work and family are closely associated with this Suit which is associated with Winter, the Element of Earth, the Letter A, the North Quarter of the Circle, and Night. The Astrological signs that correspond are Taurus, Virgo and Capricorn.

The Care and Handling of the Tarot

While many believe that the Tarot should be wrapped in a black cloth and cleansed with sea salt or another symbolic "clean" substance, i.e. holy water, oil, sunlight, the light of the full moon, I find that "bonding" with your cards is most effective in ensuring your working well with your deck.

By bonding, I mean that you should connect with your cards spiritually, on an individual basis. So if holy water is symbolic to you of purity, by all means, use this to clear any negative vibrations from your cards, or if sea salt symbolizes cleansing, use it, but choose something that to you symbolizes purity. Your deck, especially your first deck, is a spiritual tool. Treat it as such.

The cards should be treated with respect, many wrap their cards in a black cloth, black being a neutral color that does not absorb but reflects negativity. Other cartomancers prefer to wrap their cards in white, universally recognized as the color of purity. Still others use small pouches or scarves, anything you are comfortable with will do, but be sure that you handle the cards and store them in a manner which reflects respect for their status as a spiritual tool, likened to a set of rosary beads or a crucifix.

By treating the cards with respect, you will begin to recognize the spirituality within the images. The cards have absolutely no power as inanimate objects; however, if you form a physical and psychological bond with them you will empower them when you commence reading for yourself or for others.

How to Use This Journal

While utilizing this journal, record your spreads as directed and then, come back to them to record what actually happened against what you believed the cards were communicating to you. Look to see if you picked up on the wrong energy of the card if you were inaccurate, or take note of your accuracies when you intuit correctly. Be sure to make note of any actions that were taken by you that may have changed the course of events as well.

Keeping a personal Tarot Journal is a wonderful way to expand on your understanding of the cards over time. This Tarot Journal works with any Tarot Deck and is designed specifically to work with the Celtic Cross Spread.

Reading the Cards

Tarot Journal

The Celtic Cross Spread

There are many, many varied and useful Tarot Spreads. There are also multiple variations of the Celtic Cross Spread. This is one variation of the ancient Celtic Cross Spread which is useful in providing readings for self and others.

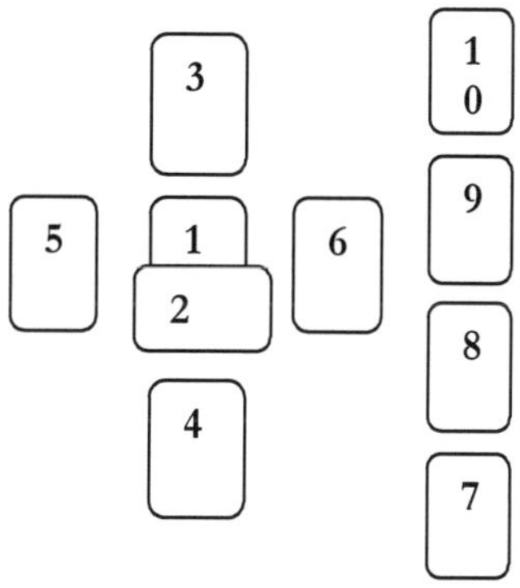

Position 1 – The Significator, the influences surrounding the Querent at this time. What is on the Querent's mind or the influences surrounding the Querent at this time?

Position 2 – The Crossing Card, forces working for or against the Querent at this time.

Position 3 – The Crowning Card, the influence that is hanging over the entire situation at this time.

Position 4 – The Base of the Matter, already a part of the Querent's experience.

Position 5 – Present and Passing, the influences that are active in the Querent's life at this time, but are exiting at the time of the reading.

Position 6 – Immediate Future, what the Querent can expect within the next two to three weeks.

Position 7 – Near Future, what the Querent can expect within the next three weeks to two months if they maintain the current path.

Position 8 – How friends and family view the situation.

Position 9 – Hopes and Fears of the Querent.

Position 10 – The Ultimate Outcome of the matter at hand if the Querent maintains the same behaviors.

The Reading

Shuffling the Cards

The key to a good Tarot Reading is the level of concentration that you maintain. Shuffle the cards while focusing on the matter you are concerned with, until the cards feel comfortable resting in your hands. Do not "ripple" them into each other as if you were dealing a hand of poker, shuffle them so that they intermix in the palm of your hand. Focus on the question that is weighing on your mind, if you have no specific question, and just want to give yourself a "general reading", allow your mind to go blank. In either case, once you are comfortable with the cards, when they feel "right" resting in your hand, cut the deck into three stacks, with your left hand, from the right to the left. The first stack you cut should be on your right, the last stack, on your left.

The reason I do this is because the left hand is ruled by the right brain, which contains our subconscious thoughts, and the left hand is directly connected to the heart, where our true desires lie.

Once you have cut the deck, pick the cards up from the right to the left, so that the first stack you cut is now the on the top of the deck. The stack that was on your left is the bottom of the deck now.

Interpreting the Spread

If you are a novice at reading, you may need to refer to the diagram while working through the positions in the spread. Record your cards by position in the journal, along with your interpretation of the card as it relates to your question and the position the card falls into. It is very important to try to make the reading flow from card to card and focus on what circumstances could make sometimes seemingly unrelated cards follow one another.

The Tarot is a spiritual and psychological tool and psychic abilities, so to speak, are not required to provide a comprehensive reading, but a strong sense of intuition is. Be open and honest with yourself, no one is going to read your journal, it's private. This will allow you to obtain a better reading and useful insight.

After you have completed recording your reading, dependent on the energy of "time" you sense, whether it be an immediate concern or a long-term goal that was the subject of your reading, go back and complete the follow up sections for each card. Answer the follow up questions honestly. Was your reading accurate or inaccurate? Was there an outside, unforeseen event that affected your situation? (Usually this is represented by the presence of a Major Arcana card in the spread). Did you misinterpret the card at first? (Cards have multiple meanings, it does happen). To understand the cards at a deep and comprehensive level, I do recommend you read my book, ***"Uncloaking The Tarot"***. Did something you did, or didn't do, affect your outcome? Record these insights, and if appropriate, read the situation again keeping your new knowledge in mind.

Were you accurate? Did what you divined from the cards occur as expected? If so, record it! Now you know you are interpreting the cards and the Celtic Cross Spread correctly and you can refer back to this interpretation when you need reinforcement for future readings.

Reversals and Dignities

Many Tarot Readers believe in reading reversed cards, this is not a method that proves accurate. All of the cards of Tarot possess both a positive and a negative energy. In order to properly interpret which energy is active, you must understand the dignity of the cards on the table.

The primary meaning of a card is what reversal readers would call "upright". The secondary energy of the card is what reversal readers would call "reversed".

Wands, which are ruled by the element of fire, are well dignified, or to be interpreted in their primary energy when they are preceded, followed by or conjunct with the element of air, which is the element of the suit of Swords, and also when falling with another Wand. Wands are ill dignified, or to be interpreted in their secondary energy, when preceded, followed by or conjunct with the elements of water and earth, Cups and Pentacles respectively.

Cups, which are ruled by the element of water, are well dignified, or to be interpreted in their primary energy when they are preceded, followed by or conjunct with the element of earth, which is the element of the suit of Pentacles, and also when falling with another Cup. Cups are ill dignified, or to be interpreted in their secondary energy, when preceded, followed by or conjunct with the elements of fire and air, Wands and Swords respectively.

Swords, which are ruled by the element of air, are well dignified, or to be interpreted in their primary energy when they are preceded, followed by or conjunct with the element of fire, which is the element of the suit of Wands, and also when falling with another Sword. Swords are ill dignified, or to be interpreted in their secondary energy, when preceded, followed by or conjunct with the elements of water and earth, Cups and Pentacles respectively.

Pentacles, which are ruled by the element of earth, are well dignified, or to be interpreted in their primary energy when they are preceded, followed by or conjunct with the element of water, which is the element of the suit of Cups, and also when falling with another Pentacle. Pentacles are ill dignified, or to be interpreted in their secondary energy, when preceded, followed by or conjunct with the elements of fire and air, Wands and Swords respectively.

Historically, reading reversals was a short cut to learning how to understand the dignities of the cards cast, however, it has been found by this cartomancers to be a highly inaccurate method. In order to ensure that reversed cards were meant to be interpreted as such, one would have to take great care to keep all seventy-eight cards of the deck facing the same way whenever handled. This is neither practical nor logical.

Ethics

It is my sincere hope that those who employ this book as a learning tool will adopt a code of ethics that is inclusive of utilizing mainstream sources of assistance for any long term or recurring problems. Most especially concerns with health, (both physical and mental), finances, legalities, or any other life situations that may require the assistance of a trained specialist. Remember, the Tarot is a guide to enhance life, not a tool that directs the course of life, free will is always available to apply to our destinies.

Reading Number: ______________________________ Date of Reading: _______________

Question Asked:

____

____

Position 1 – The Significator, the influences surrounding the Querent at this time. What is on the Querent's mind or the influences surrounding the Querent at this time?

Record card drawn and your interpretation of it:

____

____

____

____

Follow up, what actually occurred? Record how your interpretation of the card was accurate or inaccurate and why you think that happened:

____

____

____

____

Position 2 – The Crossing Card, forces working for or against the Querent at this time.

Record card drawn and your interpretation of it:

____

____

____

____

____

Follow up, what actually occurred? Record how your interpretation of the card was accurate or inaccurate and why you think that happened:

Position 3 – The Crowning Card, the influence that is hanging over the entire situation at this time.

Record card drawn and your interpretation of it:

Follow up, what actually occurred? Record how your interpretation of the card was accurate or inaccurate and why you think that happened:

Position 4 – The Base of the Matter, already a part of the Querent's experience.

Record card drawn and your interpretation of it:

Follow up, what actually occurred? Record how your interpretation of the card was accurate or inaccurate and why you think that happened:

Position 5 – Present and Passing, the influences that are active in the Querent's life at this time, but are exiting at the time of the reading.

Record card drawn and your interpretation of it:

Follow up, what actually occurred? Record how your interpretation of the card was accurate or inaccurate and why you think that happened:

Position 6 – Immediate Future, what the Querent can expect within the next two to three weeks.

Record card drawn and your interpretation of it:

Follow up, what actually occurred? Record how your interpretation of the card was accurate or inaccurate and why you think that happened:

Position 7 – Near Future, what the Querent can expect within the next three weeks to two months if they maintain the current path.

Record card drawn and your interpretation of it:

Follow up, what actually occurred? Record how your interpretation of the card was accurate or inaccurate and why you think that happened:

Position 8 – How friends and family view the situation.

Record card drawn and your interpretation of it:

Follow up, what actually occurred? Record how your interpretation of the card was accurate or inaccurate and why you think that happened:

Position 9 – Hopes and Fears of the Querent.

Record card drawn and your interpretation of it:

Follow up, what actually occurred? Record how your interpretation of the card was accurate or inaccurate and why you think that happened:

Position 10 – The Ultimate Outcome of the matter at hand if the Querent maintains the same behaviors.

Record card drawn and your interpretation of it:

Follow up, what actually occurred? Record how your interpretation of the card was accurate or inaccurate and why you think that happened:

Summarize your thoughts on this Reading:

Reading Number: ______________________________Date of Reading: _______________

Question Asked:

____

____

Position 1 – The Significator, the influences surrounding the Querent at this time. What is on the Querent's mind or the influences surrounding the Querent at this time?

Record card drawn and your interpretation of it:

____

____

____

____

Follow up, what actually occurred? Record how your interpretation of the card was accurate or inaccurate and why you think that happened:

____

____

____

____

Position 2 – The Crossing Card, forces working for or against the Querent at this time.

Record card drawn and your interpretation of it:

____

____

____

____

Follow up, what actually occurred? Record how your interpretation of the card was accurate or inaccurate and why you think that happened:

Position 3 – The Crowning Card, the influence that is hanging over the entire situation at this time.

Record card drawn and your interpretation of it:

Follow up, what actually occurred? Record how your interpretation of the card was accurate or inaccurate and why you think that happened:

Position 4 – The Base of the Matter, already a part of the Querent's experience.

Record card drawn and your interpretation of it:

Follow up, what actually occurred? Record how your interpretation of the card was accurate or inaccurate and why you think that happened:

Position 5 – Present and Passing, the influences that are active in the Querent's life at this time, but are exiting at the time of the reading.

Record card drawn and your interpretation of it:

Follow up, what actually occurred? Record how your interpretation of the card was accurate or inaccurate and why you think that happened:

Position 6 – Immediate Future, what the Querent can expect within the next two to three weeks.

Record card drawn and your interpretation of it:

Follow up, what actually occurred? Record how your interpretation of the card was accurate or inaccurate and why you think that happened:

Position 7 – Near Future, what the Querent can expect within the next three weeks to two months if they maintain the current path.

Record card drawn and your interpretation of it:

Follow up, what actually occurred? Record how your interpretation of the card was accurate or inaccurate and why you think that happened:

Position 8 – How friends and family view the situation.

Record card drawn and your interpretation of it:

Follow up, what actually occurred? Record how your interpretation of the card was accurate or inaccurate and why you think that happened:

Position 9 – Hopes and Fears of the Querent.

Record card drawn and your interpretation of it:

Follow up, what actually occurred? Record how your interpretation of the card was accurate or inaccurate and why you think that happened:

Position 10 – The Ultimate Outcome of the matter at hand if the Querent maintains the same behaviors.

Record card drawn and your interpretation of it:

Follow up, what actually occurred? Record how your interpretation of the card was accurate or inaccurate and why you think that happened:

Summarize your thoughts on this Reading:

Reading Number: ______________________________ Date of Reading: ______________

Question Asked:

____

____

Position 1 – The Significator, the influences surrounding the Querent at this time. What is on the Querent's mind or the influences surrounding the Querent at this time?

Record card drawn and your interpretation of it:

____

____

____

____

Follow up, what actually occurred? Record how your interpretation of the card was accurate or inaccurate and why you think that happened:

____

____

____

____

Position 2 – The Crossing Card, forces working for or against the Querent at this time.

Record card drawn and your interpretation of it:

____

____

____

____

Follow up, what actually occurred? Record how your interpretation of the card was accurate or inaccurate and why you think that happened:

Position 3 – The Crowning Card, the influence that is hanging over the entire situation at this time.

Record card drawn and your interpretation of it:

Follow up, what actually occurred? Record how your interpretation of the card was accurate or inaccurate and why you think that happened:

Position 4 – The Base of the Matter, already a part of the Querent's experience.

Record card drawn and your interpretation of it:

Follow up, what actually occurred? Record how your interpretation of the card was accurate or inaccurate and why you think that happened:

Position 5 – Present and Passing, the influences that are active in the Querent's life at this time, but are exiting at the time of the reading.

Record card drawn and your interpretation of it:

Follow up, what actually occurred? Record how your interpretation of the card was accurate or inaccurate and why you think that happened:

Position 6 – Immediate Future, what the Querent can expect within the next two to three weeks.

Record card drawn and your interpretation of it:

Follow up, what actually occurred? Record how your interpretation of the card was accurate or inaccurate and why you think that happened:

Position 7 – Near Future, what the Querent can expect within the next three weeks to two months if they maintain the current path.

Record card drawn and your interpretation of it:

Follow up, what actually occurred? Record how your interpretation of the card was accurate or inaccurate and why you think that happened:

Position 8 – How friends and family view the situation.

Record card drawn and your interpretation of it:

Follow up, what actually occurred? Record how your interpretation of the card was accurate or inaccurate and why you think that happened:

Position 9 – Hopes and Fears of the Querent.

Record card drawn and your interpretation of it:

Follow up, what actually occurred? Record how your interpretation of the card was accurate or inaccurate and why you think that happened:

Position 10 – The Ultimate Outcome of the matter at hand if the Querent maintains the same behaviors.

Record card drawn and your interpretation of it:

Follow up, what actually occurred? Record how your interpretation of the card was accurate or inaccurate and why you think that happened:

Summarize your thoughts on this Reading:

Reading Number: ______________________________Date of Reading: _______________

Question Asked:

____

____

Position 1 – The Significator, the influences surrounding the Querent at this time. What is on the Querent's mind or the influences surrounding the Querent at this time?

Record card drawn and your interpretation of it:

____

____

____

____

Follow up, what actually occurred? Record how your interpretation of the card was accurate or inaccurate and why you think that happened:

____

____

____

____

Position 2 – The Crossing Card, forces working for or against the Querent at this time.

Record card drawn and your interpretation of it:

____

____

____

____

Follow up, what actually occurred? Record how your interpretation of the card was accurate or inaccurate and why you think that happened:

Position 3 – The Crowning Card, the influence that is hanging over the entire situation at this time.

Record card drawn and your interpretation of it:

Follow up, what actually occurred? Record how your interpretation of the card was accurate or inaccurate and why you think that happened:

Position 4 – The Base of the Matter, already a part of the Querent's experience.

Record card drawn and your interpretation of it:

Follow up, what actually occurred? Record how your interpretation of the card was accurate or inaccurate and why you think that happened:

Position 5 – Present and Passing, the influences that are active in the Querent's life at this time, but are exiting at the time of the reading.

Record card drawn and your interpretation of it:

Follow up, what actually occurred? Record how your interpretation of the card was accurate or inaccurate and why you think that happened:

Position 6 – Immediate Future, what the Querent can expect within the next two to three weeks.

Record card drawn and your interpretation of it:

Follow up, what actually occurred? Record how your interpretation of the card was accurate or inaccurate and why you think that happened:

Position 7 – Near Future, what the Querent can expect within the next three weeks to two months if they maintain the current path.

Record card drawn and your interpretation of it:

Follow up, what actually occurred? Record how your interpretation of the card was accurate or inaccurate and why you think that happened:

Position 8 – How friends and family view the situation.

Record card drawn and your interpretation of it:

Follow up, what actually occurred? Record how your interpretation of the card was accurate or inaccurate and why you think that happened:

Position 9 – Hopes and Fears of the Querent.

Record card drawn and your interpretation of it:

Follow up, what actually occurred? Record how your interpretation of the card was accurate or inaccurate and why you think that happened:

Position 10 – The Ultimate Outcome of the matter at hand if the Querent maintains the same behaviors.

Record card drawn and your interpretation of it:

Follow up, what actually occurred? Record how your interpretation of the card was accurate or inaccurate and why you think that happened:

Summarize your thoughts on this Reading:

Reading Number: ______________________________ Date of Reading: _______________

Question Asked:

____

____

Position 1 – The Significator, the influences surrounding the Querent at this time. What is on the Querent's mind or the influences surrounding the Querent at this time?

Record card drawn and your interpretation of it:

____

____

____

____

Follow up, what actually occurred? Record how your interpretation of the card was accurate or inaccurate and why you think that happened:

____

____

____

____

Position 2 – The Crossing Card, forces working for or against the Querent at this time.

Record card drawn and your interpretation of it:

____

____

____

____

Follow up, what actually occurred? Record how your interpretation of the card was accurate or inaccurate and why you think that happened:

Position 3 – The Crowning Card, the influence that is hanging over the entire situation at this time.

Record card drawn and your interpretation of it:

Follow up, what actually occurred? Record how your interpretation of the card was accurate or inaccurate and why you think that happened:

Position 4 – The Base of the Matter, already a part of the Querent's experience.

Record card drawn and your interpretation of it:

Follow up, what actually occurred? Record how your interpretation of the card was accurate or inaccurate and why you think that happened:

Position 5 – Present and Passing, the influences that are active in the Querent's life at this time, but are exiting at the time of the reading.

Record card drawn and your interpretation of it:

Follow up, what actually occurred? Record how your interpretation of the card was accurate or inaccurate and why you think that happened:

Position 6 – Immediate Future, what the Querent can expect within the next two to three weeks.

Record card drawn and your interpretation of it:

Follow up, what actually occurred? Record how your interpretation of the card was accurate or inaccurate and why you think that happened:

Position 7 – Near Future, what the Querent can expect within the next three weeks to two months if they maintain the current path.

Record card drawn and your interpretation of it:

Follow up, what actually occurred? Record how your interpretation of the card was accurate or inaccurate and why you think that happened:

Position 8 – How friends and family view the situation.

Record card drawn and your interpretation of it:

Follow up, what actually occurred? Record how your interpretation of the card was accurate or inaccurate and why you think that happened:

Position 9 – Hopes and Fears of the Querent.

Record card drawn and your interpretation of it:

Follow up, what actually occurred? Record how your interpretation of the card was accurate or inaccurate and why you think that happened:

Position 10 – The Ultimate Outcome of the matter at hand if the Querent maintains the same behaviors.

Record card drawn and your interpretation of it:

Follow up, what actually occurred? Record how your interpretation of the card was accurate or inaccurate and why you think that happened:

Summarize your thoughts on this Reading:

Reading Number: ____________________________ Date of Reading: ______________

Question Asked:

____

____

Position 1 – The Significator, the influences surrounding the Querent at this time. What is on the Querent's mind or the influences surrounding the Querent at this time?

Record card drawn and your interpretation of it:

____

____

____

____

Follow up, what actually occurred? Record how your interpretation of the card was accurate or inaccurate and why you think that happened:

____

____

____

____

Position 2 – The Crossing Card, forces working for or against the Querent at this time.

Record card drawn and your interpretation of it:

____

____

____

____

Follow up, what actually occurred? Record how your interpretation of the card was accurate or inaccurate and why you think that happened:

Position 3 – The Crowning Card, the influence that is hanging over the entire situation at this time.

Record card drawn and your interpretation of it:

Follow up, what actually occurred? Record how your interpretation of the card was accurate or inaccurate and why you think that happened:

Position 4 – The Base of the Matter, already a part of the Querent's experience.

Record card drawn and your interpretation of it:

Follow up, what actually occurred? Record how your interpretation of the card was accurate or inaccurate and why you think that happened:

Position 5 – Present and Passing, the influences that are active in the Querent's life at this time, but are exiting at the time of the reading.

Record card drawn and your interpretation of it:

Follow up, what actually occurred? Record how your interpretation of the card was accurate or inaccurate and why you think that happened:

Position 6 – Immediate Future, what the Querent can expect within the next two to three weeks.

Record card drawn and your interpretation of it:

Follow up, what actually occurred? Record how your interpretation of the card was accurate or inaccurate and why you think that happened:

Position 7 – Near Future, what the Querent can expect within the next three weeks to two months if they maintain the current path.

Record card drawn and your interpretation of it:

Follow up, what actually occurred? Record how your interpretation of the card was accurate or inaccurate and why you think that happened:

Position 8 – How friends and family view the situation.

Record card drawn and your interpretation of it:

Follow up, what actually occurred? Record how your interpretation of the card was accurate or inaccurate and why you think that happened:

Position 9 – Hopes and Fears of the Querent.

Record card drawn and your interpretation of it:

Follow up, what actually occurred? Record how your interpretation of the card was accurate or inaccurate and why you think that happened:

Position 10 – The Ultimate Outcome of the matter at hand if the Querent maintains the same behaviors.

Record card drawn and your interpretation of it:

Follow up, what actually occurred? Record how your interpretation of the card was accurate or inaccurate and why you think that happened:

Summarize your thoughts on this Reading:

Reading Number: ______________________________ Date of Reading: ______________

Question Asked:

____

____

Position 1 – The Significator, the influences surrounding the Querent at this time. What is on the Querent's mind or the influences surrounding the Querent at this time?

Record card drawn and your interpretation of it:

____

____

____

____

Follow up, what actually occurred? Record how your interpretation of the card was accurate or inaccurate and why you think that happened:

____

____

____

____

Position 2 – The Crossing Card, forces working for or against the Querent at this time.

Record card drawn and your interpretation of it:

____

____

____

____

Follow up, what actually occurred? Record how your interpretation of the card was accurate or inaccurate and why you think that happened:

Position 3 – The Crowning Card, the influence that is hanging over the entire situation at this time.

Record card drawn and your interpretation of it:

Follow up, what actually occurred? Record how your interpretation of the card was accurate or inaccurate and why you think that happened:

Position 4 – The Base of the Matter, already a part of the Querent's experience.

Record card drawn and your interpretation of it:

Follow up, what actually occurred? Record how your interpretation of the card was accurate or inaccurate and why you think that happened:

Position 5 – Present and Passing, the influences that are active in the Querent's life at this time, but are exiting at the time of the reading.

Record card drawn and your interpretation of it:

Follow up, what actually occurred? Record how your interpretation of the card was accurate or inaccurate and why you think that happened:

Position 6 – Immediate Future, what the Querent can expect within the next two to three weeks.

Record card drawn and your interpretation of it:

Follow up, what actually occurred? Record how your interpretation of the card was accurate or inaccurate and why you think that happened:

Position 7 – Near Future, what the Querent can expect within the next three weeks to two months if they maintain the current path.

Record card drawn and your interpretation of it:

Follow up, what actually occurred? Record how your interpretation of the card was accurate or inaccurate and why you think that happened:

Position 8 – How friends and family view the situation.

Record card drawn and your interpretation of it:

Follow up, what actually occurred? Record how your interpretation of the card was accurate or inaccurate and why you think that happened:

Position 9 – Hopes and Fears of the Querent.

Record card drawn and your interpretation of it:

Follow up, what actually occurred? Record how your interpretation of the card was accurate or inaccurate and why you think that happened:

Position 10 – The Ultimate Outcome of the matter at hand if the Querent maintains the same behaviors.

Record card drawn and your interpretation of it:

Follow up, what actually occurred? Record how your interpretation of the card was accurate or inaccurate and why you think that happened:

Summarize your thoughts on this Reading:

Reading Number: ______________________________Date of Reading: _______________

Question Asked:

Position 1 – The Significator, the influences surrounding the Querent at this time. What is on the Querent's mind or the influences surrounding the Querent at this time?

Record card drawn and your interpretation of it:

Follow up, what actually occurred? Record how your interpretation of the card was accurate or inaccurate and why you think that happened:

Position 2 – The Crossing Card, forces working for or against the Querent at this time.

Record card drawn and your interpretation of it:

Follow up, what actually occurred? Record how your interpretation of the card was accurate or inaccurate and why you think that happened:

Position 3 – The Crowning Card, the influence that is hanging over the entire situation at this time.

Record card drawn and your interpretation of it:

Follow up, what actually occurred? Record how your interpretation of the card was accurate or inaccurate and why you think that happened:

Position 4 – The Base of the Matter, already a part of the Querent's experience.

Record card drawn and your interpretation of it:

Follow up, what actually occurred? Record how your interpretation of the card was accurate or inaccurate and why you think that happened:

Position 5 – Present and Passing, the influences that are active in the Querent's life at this time, but are exiting at the time of the reading.

Record card drawn and your interpretation of it:

Follow up, what actually occurred? Record how your interpretation of the card was accurate or inaccurate and why you think that happened:

Position 6 – Immediate Future, what the Querent can expect within the next two to three weeks.

Record card drawn and your interpretation of it:

Follow up, what actually occurred? Record how your interpretation of the card was accurate or inaccurate and why you think that happened:

Position 7 – Near Future, what the Querent can expect within the next three weeks to two months if they maintain the current path.

Record card drawn and your interpretation of it:

Follow up, what actually occurred? Record how your interpretation of the card was accurate or inaccurate and why you think that happened:

Position 8 – How friends and family view the situation.

Record card drawn and your interpretation of it:

Follow up, what actually occurred? Record how your interpretation of the card was accurate or inaccurate and why you think that happened:

Position 9 – Hopes and Fears of the Querent.

Record card drawn and your interpretation of it:

Follow up, what actually occurred? Record how your interpretation of the card was accurate or inaccurate and why you think that happened:

Position 10 – The Ultimate Outcome of the matter at hand if the Querent maintains the same behaviors.

Record card drawn and your interpretation of it:

Follow up, what actually occurred? Record how your interpretation of the card was accurate or inaccurate and why you think that happened:

Summarize your thoughts on this Reading:

Reading Number: ______________________________Date of Reading: _______________

Question Asked:

____

____

Position 1 – The Significator, the influences surrounding the Querent at this time. What is on the Querent's mind or the influences surrounding the Querent at this time?

Record card drawn and your interpretation of it:

____

____

____

____

Follow up, what actually occurred? Record how your interpretation of the card was accurate or inaccurate and why you think that happened:

____

____

____

____

Position 2 – The Crossing Card, forces working for or against the Querent at this time.

Record card drawn and your interpretation of it:

____

____

____

____

____

Follow up, what actually occurred? Record how your interpretation of the card was accurate or inaccurate and why you think that happened:

Position 3 – The Crowning Card, the influence that is hanging over the entire situation at this time.

Record card drawn and your interpretation of it:

Follow up, what actually occurred? Record how your interpretation of the card was accurate or inaccurate and why you think that happened:

Position 4 – The Base of the Matter, already a part of the Querent's experience.

Record card drawn and your interpretation of it:

Follow up, what actually occurred? Record how your interpretation of the card was accurate or inaccurate and why you think that happened:

Position 5 – Present and Passing, the influences that are active in the Querent's life at this time, but are exiting at the time of the reading.

Record card drawn and your interpretation of it:

Follow up, what actually occurred? Record how your interpretation of the card was accurate or inaccurate and why you think that happened:

Position 6 – Immediate Future, what the Querent can expect within the next two to three weeks.

Record card drawn and your interpretation of it:

Follow up, what actually occurred? Record how your interpretation of the card was accurate or inaccurate and why you think that happened:

Position 7 – Near Future, what the Querent can expect within the next three weeks to two months if they maintain the current path.

Record card drawn and your interpretation of it:

Follow up, what actually occurred? Record how your interpretation of the card was accurate or inaccurate and why you think that happened:

Position 8 – How friends and family view the situation.

Record card drawn and your interpretation of it:

Follow up, what actually occurred? Record how your interpretation of the card was accurate or inaccurate and why you think that happened:

Position 9 – Hopes and Fears of the Querent.

Record card drawn and your interpretation of it:

Follow up, what actually occurred? Record how your interpretation of the card was accurate or inaccurate and why you think that happened:

Position 10 – The Ultimate Outcome of the matter at hand if the Querent maintains the same behaviors.

Record card drawn and your interpretation of it:

Follow up, what actually occurred? Record how your interpretation of the card was accurate or inaccurate and why you think that happened:

Summarize your thoughts on this Reading:

Reading Number: ______________________________Date of Reading: _______________

Question Asked:

____

____

Position 1 – The Significator, the influences surrounding the Querent at this time. What is on the Querent's mind or the influences surrounding the Querent at this time?

Record card drawn and your interpretation of it:

____

____

____

____

Follow up, what actually occurred? Record how your interpretation of the card was accurate or inaccurate and why you think that happened:

____

____

____

____

Position 2 – The Crossing Card, forces working for or against the Querent at this time.

Record card drawn and your interpretation of it:

____

____

____

____

Follow up, what actually occurred? Record how your interpretation of the card was accurate or inaccurate and why you think that happened:

Position 3 – The Crowning Card, the influence that is hanging over the entire situation at this time.

Record card drawn and your interpretation of it:

Follow up, what actually occurred? Record how your interpretation of the card was accurate or inaccurate and why you think that happened:

Position 4 – The Base of the Matter, already a part of the Querent's experience.

Record card drawn and your interpretation of it:

Follow up, what actually occurred? Record how your interpretation of the card was accurate or inaccurate and why you think that happened:

Position 5 – Present and Passing, the influences that are active in the Querent's life at this time, but are exiting at the time of the reading.

Record card drawn and your interpretation of it:

Follow up, what actually occurred? Record how your interpretation of the card was accurate or inaccurate and why you think that happened:

Position 6 – Immediate Future, what the Querent can expect within the next two to three weeks.

Record card drawn and your interpretation of it:

Follow up, what actually occurred? Record how your interpretation of the card was accurate or inaccurate and why you think that happened:

Position 7 – Near Future, what the Querent can expect within the next three weeks to two months if they maintain the current path.

Record card drawn and your interpretation of it:

Follow up, what actually occurred? Record how your interpretation of the card was accurate or inaccurate and why you think that happened:

Position 8 – How friends and family view the situation.

Record card drawn and your interpretation of it:

Follow up, what actually occurred? Record how your interpretation of the card was accurate or inaccurate and why you think that happened:

Position 9 – Hopes and Fears of the Querent.

Record card drawn and your interpretation of it:

Follow up, what actually occurred? Record how your interpretation of the card was accurate or inaccurate and why you think that happened:

Position 10 – The Ultimate Outcome of the matter at hand if the Querent maintains the same behaviors.

Record card drawn and your interpretation of it:

Follow up, what actually occurred? Record how your interpretation of the card was accurate or inaccurate and why you think that happened:

Summarize your thoughts on this Reading:

Reading Number: ______________________________Date of Reading: _______________

Question Asked:

____

____

Position 1 – The Significator, the influences surrounding the Querent at this time. What is on the Querent's mind or the influences surrounding the Querent at this time?

Record card drawn and your interpretation of it:

____

____

____

____

Follow up, what actually occurred? Record how your interpretation of the card was accurate or inaccurate and why you think that happened:

____

____

____

____

Position 2 – The Crossing Card, forces working for or against the Querent at this time.

Record card drawn and your interpretation of it:

____

____

____

____

Follow up, what actually occurred? Record how your interpretation of the card was accurate or inaccurate and why you think that happened:

Position 3 – The Crowning Card, the influence that is hanging over the entire situation at this time.

Record card drawn and your interpretation of it:

Follow up, what actually occurred? Record how your interpretation of the card was accurate or inaccurate and why you think that happened:

Position 4 – The Base of the Matter, already a part of the Querent's experience.

Record card drawn and your interpretation of it:

Follow up, what actually occurred? Record how your interpretation of the card was accurate or inaccurate and why you think that happened:

Position 5 – Present and Passing, the influences that are active in the Querent's life at this time, but are exiting at the time of the reading.

Record card drawn and your interpretation of it:

Follow up, what actually occurred? Record how your interpretation of the card was accurate or inaccurate and why you think that happened:

Position 6 – Immediate Future, what the Querent can expect within the next two to three weeks.

Record card drawn and your interpretation of it:

Follow up, what actually occurred? Record how your interpretation of the card was accurate or inaccurate and why you think that happened:

Position 7 – Near Future, what the Querent can expect within the next three weeks to two months if they maintain the current path.

Record card drawn and your interpretation of it:

Follow up, what actually occurred? Record how your interpretation of the card was accurate or inaccurate and why you think that happened:

Position 8 – How friends and family view the situation.

Record card drawn and your interpretation of it:

Follow up, what actually occurred? Record how your interpretation of the card was accurate or inaccurate and why you think that happened:

Position 9 – Hopes and Fears of the Querent.

Record card drawn and your interpretation of it:

Follow up, what actually occurred? Record how your interpretation of the card was accurate or inaccurate and why you think that happened:

Position 10 – The Ultimate Outcome of the matter at hand if the Querent maintains the same behaviors.

Record card drawn and your interpretation of it:

Follow up, what actually occurred? Record how your interpretation of the card was accurate or inaccurate and why you think that happened:

Summarize your thoughts on this Reading:

Reading Number: ______________________________Date of Reading: _______________

Question Asked:

____

____

Position 1 – The Significator, the influences surrounding the Querent at this time. What is on the Querent's mind or the influences surrounding the Querent at this time?

Record card drawn and your interpretation of it:

____

____

____

____

Follow up, what actually occurred? Record how your interpretation of the card was accurate or inaccurate and why you think that happened:

____

____

____

____

Position 2 – The Crossing Card, forces working for or against the Querent at this time.

Record card drawn and your interpretation of it:

____

____

____

____

Follow up, what actually occurred? Record how your interpretation of the card was accurate or inaccurate and why you think that happened:

Position 3 – The Crowning Card, the influence that is hanging over the entire situation at this time.

Record card drawn and your interpretation of it:

Follow up, what actually occurred? Record how your interpretation of the card was accurate or inaccurate and why you think that happened:

Position 4 – The Base of the Matter, already a part of the Querent's experience.

Record card drawn and your interpretation of it:

Follow up, what actually occurred? Record how your interpretation of the card was accurate or inaccurate and why you think that happened:

Position 5 – Present and Passing, the influences that are active in the Querent's life at this time, but are exiting at the time of the reading.

Record card drawn and your interpretation of it:

Follow up, what actually occurred? Record how your interpretation of the card was accurate or inaccurate and why you think that happened:

Position 6 – Immediate Future, what the Querent can expect within the next two to three weeks.

Record card drawn and your interpretation of it:

Follow up, what actually occurred? Record how your interpretation of the card was accurate or inaccurate and why you think that happened:

Position 7 – Near Future, what the Querent can expect within the next three weeks to two months if they maintain the current path.

Record card drawn and your interpretation of it:

Follow up, what actually occurred? Record how your interpretation of the card was accurate or inaccurate and why you think that happened:

Position 8 – How friends and family view the situation.

Record card drawn and your interpretation of it:

Follow up, what actually occurred? Record how your interpretation of the card was accurate or inaccurate and why you think that happened:

Position 9 – Hopes and Fears of the Querent.

Record card drawn and your interpretation of it:

Follow up, what actually occurred? Record how your interpretation of the card was accurate or inaccurate and why you think that happened:

Position 10 – The Ultimate Outcome of the matter at hand if the Querent maintains the same behaviors.

Record card drawn and your interpretation of it:

Follow up, what actually occurred? Record how your interpretation of the card was accurate or inaccurate and why you think that happened:

Summarize your thoughts on this Reading:

Reading Number: ______________________________Date of Reading: ______________

Question Asked:

____

____

Position 1 – The Significator, the influences surrounding the Querent at this time. What is on the Querent's mind or the influences surrounding the Querent at this time?

Record card drawn and your interpretation of it:

____

____

____

____

Follow up, what actually occurred? Record how your interpretation of the card was accurate or inaccurate and why you think that happened:

____

____

____

____

Position 2 – The Crossing Card, forces working for or against the Querent at this time.

Record card drawn and your interpretation of it:

____

____

____

____

____

Follow up, what actually occurred? Record how your interpretation of the card was accurate or inaccurate and why you think that happened:

Position 3 – The Crowning Card, the influence that is hanging over the entire situation at this time.

Record card drawn and your interpretation of it:

Follow up, what actually occurred? Record how your interpretation of the card was accurate or inaccurate and why you think that happened:

Position 4 – The Base of the Matter, already a part of the Querent's experience.

Record card drawn and your interpretation of it:

Follow up, what actually occurred? Record how your interpretation of the card was accurate or inaccurate and why you think that happened:

Position 5 – Present and Passing, the influences that are active in the Querent's life at this time, but are exiting at the time of the reading.

Record card drawn and your interpretation of it:

Follow up, what actually occurred? Record how your interpretation of the card was accurate or inaccurate and why you think that happened:

Position 6 – Immediate Future, what the Querent can expect within the next two to three weeks.

Record card drawn and your interpretation of it:

Follow up, what actually occurred? Record how your interpretation of the card was accurate or inaccurate and why you think that happened:

Position 7 – Near Future, what the Querent can expect within the next three weeks to two months if they maintain the current path.

Record card drawn and your interpretation of it:

Follow up, what actually occurred? Record how your interpretation of the card was accurate or inaccurate and why you think that happened:

Position 8 – How friends and family view the situation.

Record card drawn and your interpretation of it:

Follow up, what actually occurred? Record how your interpretation of the card was accurate or inaccurate and why you think that happened:

Position 9 – Hopes and Fears of the Querent.

Record card drawn and your interpretation of it:

Follow up, what actually occurred? Record how your interpretation of the card was accurate or inaccurate and why you think that happened:

Position 10 – The Ultimate Outcome of the matter at hand if the Querent maintains the same behaviors.

Record card drawn and your interpretation of it:

Follow up, what actually occurred? Record how your interpretation of the card was accurate or inaccurate and why you think that happened:

Summarize your thoughts on this Reading:

Reading Number: ______________________________ Date of Reading: ______________

Question Asked:

____

____

Position 1 – The Significator, the influences surrounding the Querent at this time. What is on the Querent's mind or the influences surrounding the Querent at this time?

Record card drawn and your interpretation of it:

____

____

____

____

Follow up, what actually occurred? Record how your interpretation of the card was accurate or inaccurate and why you think that happened:

____

____

____

____

Position 2 – The Crossing Card, forces working for or against the Querent at this time.

Record card drawn and your interpretation of it:

____

____

____

____

____

Follow up, what actually occurred? Record how your interpretation of the card was accurate or inaccurate and why you think that happened:

Position 3 – The Crowning Card, the influence that is hanging over the entire situation at this time.

Record card drawn and your interpretation of it:

Follow up, what actually occurred? Record how your interpretation of the card was accurate or inaccurate and why you think that happened:

Position 4 – The Base of the Matter, already a part of the Querent's experience.

Record card drawn and your interpretation of it:

Follow up, what actually occurred? Record how your interpretation of the card was accurate or inaccurate and why you think that happened:

Position 5 – Present and Passing, the influences that are active in the Querent's life at this time, but are exiting at the time of the reading.

Record card drawn and your interpretation of it:

Follow up, what actually occurred? Record how your interpretation of the card was accurate or inaccurate and why you think that happened:

Position 6 – Immediate Future, what the Querent can expect within the next two to three weeks.

Record card drawn and your interpretation of it:

Follow up, what actually occurred? Record how your interpretation of the card was accurate or inaccurate and why you think that happened:

Position 7 – Near Future, what the Querent can expect within the next three weeks to two months if they maintain the current path.

Record card drawn and your interpretation of it:

Follow up, what actually occurred? Record how your interpretation of the card was accurate or inaccurate and why you think that happened:

Position 8 – How friends and family view the situation.

Record card drawn and your interpretation of it:

Follow up, what actually occurred? Record how your interpretation of the card was accurate or inaccurate and why you think that happened:

Position 9 – Hopes and Fears of the Querent.

Record card drawn and your interpretation of it:

Follow up, what actually occurred? Record how your interpretation of the card was accurate or inaccurate and why you think that happened:

Position 10 – The Ultimate Outcome of the matter at hand if the Querent maintains the same behaviors.

Record card drawn and your interpretation of it:

Follow up, what actually occurred? Record how your interpretation of the card was accurate or inaccurate and why you think that happened:

Summarize your thoughts on this Reading:

Reading Number: ______________________ Date of Reading: __________

Question Asked:

____

____

Position 1 – The Significator, the influences surrounding the Querent at this time. What is on the Querent's mind or the influences surrounding the Querent at this time?

Record card drawn and your interpretation of it:

____

____

____

____

Follow up, what actually occurred? Record how your interpretation of the card was accurate or inaccurate and why you think that happened:

____

____

____

____

Position 2 – The Crossing Card, forces working for or against the Querent at this time.

Record card drawn and your interpretation of it:

____

____

____

____

Follow up, what actually occurred? Record how your interpretation of the card was accurate or inaccurate and why you think that happened:

Position 3 – The Crowning Card, the influence that is hanging over the entire situation at this time.

Record card drawn and your interpretation of it:

Follow up, what actually occurred? Record how your interpretation of the card was accurate or inaccurate and why you think that happened:

Position 4 – The Base of the Matter, already a part of the Querent's experience.

Record card drawn and your interpretation of it:

Follow up, what actually occurred? Record how your interpretation of the card was accurate or inaccurate and why you think that happened:

Position 5 – Present and Passing, the influences that are active in the Querent's life at this time, but are exiting at the time of the reading.

Record card drawn and your interpretation of it:

Follow up, what actually occurred? Record how your interpretation of the card was accurate or inaccurate and why you think that happened:

Position 6 – Immediate Future, what the Querent can expect within the next two to three weeks.

Record card drawn and your interpretation of it:

Follow up, what actually occurred? Record how your interpretation of the card was accurate or inaccurate and why you think that happened:

Position 7 – Near Future, what the Querent can expect within the next three weeks to two months if they maintain the current path.

Record card drawn and your interpretation of it:

Follow up, what actually occurred? Record how your interpretation of the card was accurate or inaccurate and why you think that happened:

Position 8 – How friends and family view the situation.

Record card drawn and your interpretation of it:

Follow up, what actually occurred? Record how your interpretation of the card was accurate or inaccurate and why you think that happened:

Position 9 – Hopes and Fears of the Querent.

Record card drawn and your interpretation of it:

Follow up, what actually occurred? Record how your interpretation of the card was accurate or inaccurate and why you think that happened:

Position 10 – The Ultimate Outcome of the matter at hand if the Querent maintains the same behaviors.

Record card drawn and your interpretation of it:

Follow up, what actually occurred? Record how your interpretation of the card was accurate or inaccurate and why you think that happened:

Summarize your thoughts on this Reading:

Reading Number: ______________________________Date of Reading: _______________

Question Asked:

Position 1 – The Significator, the influences surrounding the Querent at this time. What is on the Querent's mind or the influences surrounding the Querent at this time?

Record card drawn and your interpretation of it:

Follow up, what actually occurred? Record how your interpretation of the card was accurate or inaccurate and why you think that happened:

Position 2 – The Crossing Card, forces working for or against the Querent at this time.

Record card drawn and your interpretation of it:

Follow up, what actually occurred? Record how your interpretation of the card was accurate or inaccurate and why you think that happened:

Position 3 – The Crowning Card, the influence that is hanging over the entire situation at this time.

Record card drawn and your interpretation of it:

Follow up, what actually occurred? Record how your interpretation of the card was accurate or inaccurate and why you think that happened:

Position 4 – The Base of the Matter, already a part of the Querent's experience.

Record card drawn and your interpretation of it:

Follow up, what actually occurred? Record how your interpretation of the card was accurate or inaccurate and why you think that happened:

Position 5 – Present and Passing, the influences that are active in the Querent's life at this time, but are exiting at the time of the reading.

Record card drawn and your interpretation of it:

Follow up, what actually occurred? Record how your interpretation of the card was accurate or inaccurate and why you think that happened:

Position 6 – Immediate Future, what the Querent can expect within the next two to three weeks.

Record card drawn and your interpretation of it:

Follow up, what actually occurred? Record how your interpretation of the card was accurate or inaccurate and why you think that happened:

Position 7 – Near Future, what the Querent can expect within the next three weeks to two months if they maintain the current path.

Record card drawn and your interpretation of it:

Follow up, what actually occurred? Record how your interpretation of the card was accurate or inaccurate and why you think that happened:

Position 8 – How friends and family view the situation.

Record card drawn and your interpretation of it:

Follow up, what actually occurred? Record how your interpretation of the card was accurate or inaccurate and why you think that happened:

Position 9 – Hopes and Fears of the Querent.

Record card drawn and your interpretation of it:

Follow up, what actually occurred? Record how your interpretation of the card was accurate or inaccurate and why you think that happened:

Position 10 – The Ultimate Outcome of the matter at hand if the Querent maintains the same behaviors.

Record card drawn and your interpretation of it:

Follow up, what actually occurred? Record how your interpretation of the card was accurate or inaccurate and why you think that happened:

Summarize your thoughts on this Reading:

Reading Number: ______________________________ Date of Reading: ______________

Question Asked:

Position 1 – The Significator, the influences surrounding the Querent at this time. What is on the Querent's mind or the influences surrounding the Querent at this time?

Record card drawn and your interpretation of it:

Follow up, what actually occurred? Record how your interpretation of the card was accurate or inaccurate and why you think that happened:

Position 2 – The Crossing Card, forces working for or against the Querent at this time.

Record card drawn and your interpretation of it:

Follow up, what actually occurred? Record how your interpretation of the card was accurate or inaccurate and why you think that happened:

Position 3 – The Crowning Card, the influence that is hanging over the entire situation at this time.

Record card drawn and your interpretation of it:

Follow up, what actually occurred? Record how your interpretation of the card was accurate or inaccurate and why you think that happened:

Position 4 – The Base of the Matter, already a part of the Querent's experience.

Record card drawn and your interpretation of it:

Follow up, what actually occurred? Record how your interpretation of the card was accurate or inaccurate and why you think that happened:

Position 5 – Present and Passing, the influences that are active in the Querent's life at this time, but are exiting at the time of the reading.

Record card drawn and your interpretation of it:

Follow up, what actually occurred? Record how your interpretation of the card was accurate or inaccurate and why you think that happened:

Position 6 – Immediate Future, what the Querent can expect within the next two to three weeks.

Record card drawn and your interpretation of it:

Follow up, what actually occurred? Record how your interpretation of the card was accurate or inaccurate and why you think that happened:

Position 7 – Near Future, what the Querent can expect within the next three weeks to two months if they maintain the current path.

Record card drawn and your interpretation of it:

Follow up, what actually occurred? Record how your interpretation of the card was accurate or inaccurate and why you think that happened:

Position 8 – How friends and family view the situation.

Record card drawn and your interpretation of it:

Follow up, what actually occurred? Record how your interpretation of the card was accurate or inaccurate and why you think that happened:

Position 9 – Hopes and Fears of the Querent.

Record card drawn and your interpretation of it:

Follow up, what actually occurred? Record how your interpretation of the card was accurate or inaccurate and why you think that happened:

Position 10 – The Ultimate Outcome of the matter at hand if the Querent maintains the same behaviors.

Record card drawn and your interpretation of it:

Follow up, what actually occurred? Record how your interpretation of the card was accurate or inaccurate and why you think that happened:

Summarize your thoughts on this Reading:

Reading Number: ______________________________Date of Reading: ______________

Question Asked:

____

____

Position 1 – The Significator, the influences surrounding the Querent at this time. What is on the Querent's mind or the influences surrounding the Querent at this time?

Record card drawn and your interpretation of it:

____

____

____

____

Follow up, what actually occurred? Record how your interpretation of the card was accurate or inaccurate and why you think that happened:

____

____

____

____

Position 2 – The Crossing Card, forces working for or against the Querent at this time.

Record card drawn and your interpretation of it:

____

____

____

____

Follow up, what actually occurred? Record how your interpretation of the card was accurate or inaccurate and why you think that happened:

Position 3 – The Crowning Card, the influence that is hanging over the entire situation at this time.

Record card drawn and your interpretation of it:

Follow up, what actually occurred? Record how your interpretation of the card was accurate or inaccurate and why you think that happened:

Position 4 – The Base of the Matter, already a part of the Querent's experience.

Record card drawn and your interpretation of it:

Follow up, what actually occurred? Record how your interpretation of the card was accurate or inaccurate and why you think that happened:

Position 5 – Present and Passing, the influences that are active in the Querent's life at this time, but are exiting at the time of the reading.

Record card drawn and your interpretation of it:

Follow up, what actually occurred? Record how your interpretation of the card was accurate or inaccurate and why you think that happened:

Position 6 – Immediate Future, what the Querent can expect within the next two to three weeks.

Record card drawn and your interpretation of it:

Follow up, what actually occurred? Record how your interpretation of the card was accurate or inaccurate and why you think that happened:

Position 7 – Near Future, what the Querent can expect within the next three weeks to two months if they maintain the current path.

Record card drawn and your interpretation of it:

Follow up, what actually occurred? Record how your interpretation of the card was accurate or inaccurate and why you think that happened:

Position 8 – How friends and family view the situation.

Record card drawn and your interpretation of it:

Follow up, what actually occurred? Record how your interpretation of the card was accurate or inaccurate and why you think that happened:

Position 9 – Hopes and Fears of the Querent.

Record card drawn and your interpretation of it:

Follow up, what actually occurred? Record how your interpretation of the card was accurate or inaccurate and why you think that happened:

Position 10 – The Ultimate Outcome of the matter at hand if the Querent maintains the same behaviors.

Record card drawn and your interpretation of it:

Follow up, what actually occurred? Record how your interpretation of the card was accurate or inaccurate and why you think that happened:

Summarize your thoughts on this Reading:

Reading Number: ______________________________Date of Reading: _______________

Question Asked:

____

____

Position 1 – The Significator, the influences surrounding the Querent at this time. What is on the Querent's mind or the influences surrounding the Querent at this time?

Record card drawn and your interpretation of it:

____

____

____

____

Follow up, what actually occurred? Record how your interpretation of the card was accurate or inaccurate and why you think that happened:

____

____

____

____

Position 2 – The Crossing Card, forces working for or against the Querent at this time.

Record card drawn and your interpretation of it:

____

____

____

____

Follow up, what actually occurred? Record how your interpretation of the card was accurate or inaccurate and why you think that happened:

Position 3 – The Crowning Card, the influence that is hanging over the entire situation at this time.

Record card drawn and your interpretation of it:

Follow up, what actually occurred? Record how your interpretation of the card was accurate or inaccurate and why you think that happened:

Position 4 – The Base of the Matter, already a part of the Querent's experience.

Record card drawn and your interpretation of it:

Follow up, what actually occurred? Record how your interpretation of the card was accurate or inaccurate and why you think that happened:

Position 5 – Present and Passing, the influences that are active in the Querent's life at this time, but are exiting at the time of the reading.

Record card drawn and your interpretation of it:

Follow up, what actually occurred? Record how your interpretation of the card was accurate or inaccurate and why you think that happened:

Position 6 – Immediate Future, what the Querent can expect within the next two to three weeks.

Record card drawn and your interpretation of it:

Follow up, what actually occurred? Record how your interpretation of the card was accurate or inaccurate and why you think that happened:

Position 7 – Near Future, what the Querent can expect within the next three weeks to two months if they maintain the current path.

Record card drawn and your interpretation of it:

Follow up, what actually occurred? Record how your interpretation of the card was accurate or inaccurate and why you think that happened:

Position 8 – How friends and family view the situation.

Record card drawn and your interpretation of it:

Follow up, what actually occurred? Record how your interpretation of the card was accurate or inaccurate and why you think that happened:

Position 9 – Hopes and Fears of the Querent.

Record card drawn and your interpretation of it:

Follow up, what actually occurred? Record how your interpretation of the card was accurate or inaccurate and why you think that happened:

Position 10 – The Ultimate Outcome of the matter at hand if the Querent maintains the same behaviors.

Record card drawn and your interpretation of it:

Follow up, what actually occurred? Record how your interpretation of the card was accurate or inaccurate and why you think that happened:

Summarize your thoughts on this Reading:

Reading Number: ______________________________Date of Reading: ______________

Question Asked:

____

____

Position 1 – The Significator, the influences surrounding the Querent at this time. What is on the Querent's mind or the influences surrounding the Querent at this time?

Record card drawn and your interpretation of it:

____

____

____

____

Follow up, what actually occurred? Record how your interpretation of the card was accurate or inaccurate and why you think that happened:

____

____

____

____

Position 2 – The Crossing Card, forces working for or against the Querent at this time.

Record card drawn and your interpretation of it:

____

____

____

____

Follow up, what actually occurred? Record how your interpretation of the card was accurate or inaccurate and why you think that happened:

Position 3 – The Crowning Card, the influence that is hanging over the entire situation at this time.

Record card drawn and your interpretation of it:

Follow up, what actually occurred? Record how your interpretation of the card was accurate or inaccurate and why you think that happened:

Position 4 – The Base of the Matter, already a part of the Querent's experience.

Record card drawn and your interpretation of it:

Follow up, what actually occurred? Record how your interpretation of the card was accurate or inaccurate and why you think that happened:

Position 5 – Present and Passing, the influences that are active in the Querent's life at this time, but are exiting at the time of the reading.

Record card drawn and your interpretation of it:

Follow up, what actually occurred? Record how your interpretation of the card was accurate or inaccurate and why you think that happened:

Position 6 – Immediate Future, what the Querent can expect within the next two to three weeks.

Record card drawn and your interpretation of it:

Follow up, what actually occurred? Record how your interpretation of the card was accurate or inaccurate and why you think that happened:

Position 7 – Near Future, what the Querent can expect within the next three weeks to two months if they maintain the current path.

Record card drawn and your interpretation of it:

Follow up, what actually occurred? Record how your interpretation of the card was accurate or inaccurate and why you think that happened:

Position 8 – How friends and family view the situation.

Record card drawn and your interpretation of it:

Follow up, what actually occurred? Record how your interpretation of the card was accurate or inaccurate and why you think that happened:

Position 9 – Hopes and Fears of the Querent.

Record card drawn and your interpretation of it:

Follow up, what actually occurred? Record how your interpretation of the card was accurate or inaccurate and why you think that happened:

Position 10 – The Ultimate Outcome of the matter at hand if the Querent maintains the same behaviors.

Record card drawn and your interpretation of it:

Follow up, what actually occurred? Record how your interpretation of the card was accurate or inaccurate and why you think that happened:

Summarize your thoughts on this Reading:

Reading Number: ______________________________Date of Reading: ______________

Question Asked:

____

____

Position 1 – The Significator, the influences surrounding the Querent at this time. What is on the Querent's mind or the influences surrounding the Querent at this time?

Record card drawn and your interpretation of it:

____

____

____

____

Follow up, what actually occurred? Record how your interpretation of the card was accurate or inaccurate and why you think that happened:

____

____

____

____

Position 2 – The Crossing Card, forces working for or against the Querent at this time.

Record card drawn and your interpretation of it:

____

____

____

____

Follow up, what actually occurred? Record how your interpretation of the card was accurate or inaccurate and why you think that happened:

Position 3 – The Crowning Card, the influence that is hanging over the entire situation at this time.

Record card drawn and your interpretation of it:

Follow up, what actually occurred? Record how your interpretation of the card was accurate or inaccurate and why you think that happened:

Position 4 – The Base of the Matter, already a part of the Querent's experience.

Record card drawn and your interpretation of it:

Follow up, what actually occurred? Record how your interpretation of the card was accurate or inaccurate and why you think that happened:

Position 5 – Present and Passing, the influences that are active in the Querent's life at this time, but are exiting at the time of the reading.

Record card drawn and your interpretation of it:

Follow up, what actually occurred? Record how your interpretation of the card was accurate or inaccurate and why you think that happened:

Position 6 – Immediate Future, what the Querent can expect within the next two to three weeks.

Record card drawn and your interpretation of it:

Follow up, what actually occurred? Record how your interpretation of the card was accurate or inaccurate and why you think that happened:

Position 7 – Near Future, what the Querent can expect within the next three weeks to two months if they maintain the current path.

Record card drawn and your interpretation of it:

Follow up, what actually occurred? Record how your interpretation of the card was accurate or inaccurate and why you think that happened:

Position 8 – How friends and family view the situation.

Record card drawn and your interpretation of it:

Follow up, what actually occurred? Record how your interpretation of the card was accurate or inaccurate and why you think that happened:

Position 9 – Hopes and Fears of the Querent.

Record card drawn and your interpretation of it:

Follow up, what actually occurred? Record how your interpretation of the card was accurate or inaccurate and why you think that happened:

Position 10 – The Ultimate Outcome of the matter at hand if the Querent maintains the same behaviors.

Record card drawn and your interpretation of it:

Follow up, what actually occurred? Record how your interpretation of the card was accurate or inaccurate and why you think that happened:

Summarize your thoughts on this Reading:

Reading Number: ______________________________Date of Reading: _______________

Question Asked:

____

____

Position 1 – The Significator, the influences surrounding the Querent at this time. What is on the Querent's mind or the influences surrounding the Querent at this time?

Record card drawn and your interpretation of it:

____

____

____

____

Follow up, what actually occurred? Record how your interpretation of the card was accurate or inaccurate and why you think that happened:

____

____

____

____

Position 2 – The Crossing Card, forces working for or against the Querent at this time.

Record card drawn and your interpretation of it:

____

____

____

____

Follow up, what actually occurred? Record how your interpretation of the card was accurate or inaccurate and why you think that happened:

Position 3 – The Crowning Card, the influence that is hanging over the entire situation at this time.

Record card drawn and your interpretation of it:

Follow up, what actually occurred? Record how your interpretation of the card was accurate or inaccurate and why you think that happened:

Position 4 – The Base of the Matter, already a part of the Querent's experience.

Record card drawn and your interpretation of it:

Follow up, what actually occurred? Record how your interpretation of the card was accurate or inaccurate and why you think that happened:

Position 5 – Present and Passing, the influences that are active in the Querent's life at this time, but are exiting at the time of the reading.

Record card drawn and your interpretation of it:

Follow up, what actually occurred? Record how your interpretation of the card was accurate or inaccurate and why you think that happened:

Position 6 – Immediate Future, what the Querent can expect within the next two to three weeks.

Record card drawn and your interpretation of it:

Follow up, what actually occurred? Record how your interpretation of the card was accurate or inaccurate and why you think that happened:

Position 7 – Near Future, what the Querent can expect within the next three weeks to two months if they maintain the current path.

Record card drawn and your interpretation of it:

Follow up, what actually occurred? Record how your interpretation of the card was accurate or inaccurate and why you think that happened:

Position 8 – How friends and family view the situation.

Record card drawn and your interpretation of it:

Follow up, what actually occurred? Record how your interpretation of the card was accurate or inaccurate and why you think that happened:

Position 9 – Hopes and Fears of the Querent.

Record card drawn and your interpretation of it:

Follow up, what actually occurred? Record how your interpretation of the card was accurate or inaccurate and why you think that happened:

Position 10 – The Ultimate Outcome of the matter at hand if the Querent maintains the same behaviors.

Record card drawn and your interpretation of it:

Follow up, what actually occurred? Record how your interpretation of the card was accurate or inaccurate and why you think that happened:

Summarize your thoughts on this Reading:

Reading Number: ______________________________Date of Reading: _______________

Question Asked:

____

____

Position 1 – The Significator, the influences surrounding the Querent at this time. What is on the Querent's mind or the influences surrounding the Querent at this time?

Record card drawn and your interpretation of it:

____

____

____

____

Follow up, what actually occurred? Record how your interpretation of the card was accurate or inaccurate and why you think that happened:

____

____

____

____

Position 2 – The Crossing Card, forces working for or against the Querent at this time.

Record card drawn and your interpretation of it:

____

____

____

____

Follow up, what actually occurred? Record how your interpretation of the card was accurate or inaccurate and why you think that happened:

Position 3 – The Crowning Card, the influence that is hanging over the entire situation at this time.

Record card drawn and your interpretation of it:

Follow up, what actually occurred? Record how your interpretation of the card was accurate or inaccurate and why you think that happened:

Position 4 – The Base of the Matter, already a part of the Querent's experience.

Record card drawn and your interpretation of it:

Follow up, what actually occurred? Record how your interpretation of the card was accurate or inaccurate and why you think that happened:

Position 5 – Present and Passing, the influences that are active in the Querent's life at this time, but are exiting at the time of the reading.

Record card drawn and your interpretation of it:

Follow up, what actually occurred? Record how your interpretation of the card was accurate or inaccurate and why you think that happened:

Position 6 – Immediate Future, what the Querent can expect within the next two to three weeks.

Record card drawn and your interpretation of it:

Follow up, what actually occurred? Record how your interpretation of the card was accurate or inaccurate and why you think that happened:

Position 7 – Near Future, what the Querent can expect within the next three weeks to two months if they maintain the current path.

Record card drawn and your interpretation of it:

Follow up, what actually occurred? Record how your interpretation of the card was accurate or inaccurate and why you think that happened:

Position 8 – How friends and family view the situation.

Record card drawn and your interpretation of it:

Follow up, what actually occurred? Record how your interpretation of the card was accurate or inaccurate and why you think that happened:

Position 9 – Hopes and Fears of the Querent.

Record card drawn and your interpretation of it:

Follow up, what actually occurred? Record how your interpretation of the card was accurate or inaccurate and why you think that happened:

Position 10 – The Ultimate Outcome of the matter at hand if the Querent maintains the same behaviors.

Record card drawn and your interpretation of it:

Follow up, what actually occurred? Record how your interpretation of the card was accurate or inaccurate and why you think that happened:

Summarize your thoughts on this Reading:

Reading Number: ____________________________Date of Reading: _____________

Question Asked:

____

____

Position 1 – The Significator, the influences surrounding the Querent at this time. What is on the Querent's mind or the influences surrounding the Querent at this time?

Record card drawn and your interpretation of it:

____

____

____

____

Follow up, what actually occurred? Record how your interpretation of the card was accurate or inaccurate and why you think that happened:

____

____

____

____

Position 2 – The Crossing Card, forces working for or against the Querent at this time.

Record card drawn and your interpretation of it:

____

____

____

____

Follow up, what actually occurred? Record how your interpretation of the card was accurate or inaccurate and why you think that happened:

Position 3 – The Crowning Card, the influence that is hanging over the entire situation at this time.

Record card drawn and your interpretation of it:

Follow up, what actually occurred? Record how your interpretation of the card was accurate or inaccurate and why you think that happened:

Position 4 – The Base of the Matter, already a part of the Querent's experience.

Record card drawn and your interpretation of it:

Follow up, what actually occurred? Record how your interpretation of the card was accurate or inaccurate and why you think that happened:

Position 5 – Present and Passing, the influences that are active in the Querent's life at this time, but are exiting at the time of the reading.

Record card drawn and your interpretation of it:

Follow up, what actually occurred? Record how your interpretation of the card was accurate or inaccurate and why you think that happened:

Position 6 – Immediate Future, what the Querent can expect within the next two to three weeks.

Record card drawn and your interpretation of it:

Follow up, what actually occurred? Record how your interpretation of the card was accurate or inaccurate and why you think that happened:

Position 7 – Near Future, what the Querent can expect within the next three weeks to two months if they maintain the current path.

Record card drawn and your interpretation of it:

Follow up, what actually occurred? Record how your interpretation of the card was accurate or inaccurate and why you think that happened:

Position 8 – How friends and family view the situation.

Record card drawn and your interpretation of it:

Follow up, what actually occurred? Record how your interpretation of the card was accurate or inaccurate and why you think that happened:

Position 9 – Hopes and Fears of the Querent.

Record card drawn and your interpretation of it:

Follow up, what actually occurred? Record how your interpretation of the card was accurate or inaccurate and why you think that happened:

Position 10 – The Ultimate Outcome of the matter at hand if the Querent maintains the same behaviors.

Record card drawn and your interpretation of it:

Follow up, what actually occurred? Record how your interpretation of the card was accurate or inaccurate and why you think that happened:

Summarize your thoughts on this Reading:

Reading Number: ______________________________ Date of Reading: ______________

Question Asked:

____

____

Position 1 – The Significator, the influences surrounding the Querent at this time. What is on the Querent's mind or the influences surrounding the Querent at this time?

Record card drawn and your interpretation of it:

____

____

____

____

Follow up, what actually occurred? Record how your interpretation of the card was accurate or inaccurate and why you think that happened:

____

____

____

____

Position 2 – The Crossing Card, forces working for or against the Querent at this time.

Record card drawn and your interpretation of it:

____

____

____

____

Follow up, what actually occurred? Record how your interpretation of the card was accurate or inaccurate and why you think that happened:

Position 3 – The Crowning Card, the influence that is hanging over the entire situation at this time.

Record card drawn and your interpretation of it:

Follow up, what actually occurred? Record how your interpretation of the card was accurate or inaccurate and why you think that happened:

Position 4 – The Base of the Matter, already a part of the Querent's experience.

Record card drawn and your interpretation of it:

Follow up, what actually occurred? Record how your interpretation of the card was accurate or inaccurate and why you think that happened:

Position 5 – Present and Passing, the influences that are active in the Querent's life at this time, but are exiting at the time of the reading.

Record card drawn and your interpretation of it:

Follow up, what actually occurred? Record how your interpretation of the card was accurate or inaccurate and why you think that happened:

Position 6 – Immediate Future, what the Querent can expect within the next two to three weeks.

Record card drawn and your interpretation of it:

Follow up, what actually occurred? Record how your interpretation of the card was accurate or inaccurate and why you think that happened:

Position 7 – Near Future, what the Querent can expect within the next three weeks to two months if they maintain the current path.

Record card drawn and your interpretation of it:

Follow up, what actually occurred? Record how your interpretation of the card was accurate or inaccurate and why you think that happened:

Position 8 – How friends and family view the situation.

Record card drawn and your interpretation of it:

Follow up, what actually occurred? Record how your interpretation of the card was accurate or inaccurate and why you think that happened:

Position 9 – Hopes and Fears of the Querent.

Record card drawn and your interpretation of it:

Follow up, what actually occurred? Record how your interpretation of the card was accurate or inaccurate and why you think that happened:

Position 10 – The Ultimate Outcome of the matter at hand if the Querent maintains the same behaviors.

Record card drawn and your interpretation of it:

Follow up, what actually occurred? Record how your interpretation of the card was accurate or inaccurate and why you think that happened:

Summarize your thoughts on this Reading:

Reading Number: ______________________________ Date of Reading: _______________

Question Asked:

____

____

Position 1 – The Significator, the influences surrounding the Querent at this time. What is on the Querent's mind or the influences surrounding the Querent at this time?

Record card drawn and your interpretation of it:

____

____

____

____

Follow up, what actually occurred? Record how your interpretation of the card was accurate or inaccurate and why you think that happened:

____

____

____

____

Position 2 – The Crossing Card, forces working for or against the Querent at this time.

Record card drawn and your interpretation of it:

____

____

____

____

Follow up, what actually occurred? Record how your interpretation of the card was accurate or inaccurate and why you think that happened:

Position 3 – The Crowning Card, the influence that is hanging over the entire situation at this time.

Record card drawn and your interpretation of it:

Follow up, what actually occurred? Record how your interpretation of the card was accurate or inaccurate and why you think that happened:

Position 4 – The Base of the Matter, already a part of the Querent's experience.

Record card drawn and your interpretation of it:

Follow up, what actually occurred? Record how your interpretation of the card was accurate or inaccurate and why you think that happened:

Position 5 – Present and Passing, the influences that are active in the Querent's life at this time, but are exiting at the time of the reading.

Record card drawn and your interpretation of it:

Follow up, what actually occurred? Record how your interpretation of the card was accurate or inaccurate and why you think that happened:

Position 6 – Immediate Future, what the Querent can expect within the next two to three weeks.

Record card drawn and your interpretation of it:

Follow up, what actually occurred? Record how your interpretation of the card was accurate or inaccurate and why you think that happened:

Position 7 – Near Future, what the Querent can expect within the next three weeks to two months if they maintain the current path.

Record card drawn and your interpretation of it:

Follow up, what actually occurred? Record how your interpretation of the card was accurate or inaccurate and why you think that happened:

Position 8 – How friends and family view the situation.

Record card drawn and your interpretation of it:

Follow up, what actually occurred? Record how your interpretation of the card was accurate or inaccurate and why you think that happened:

Position 9 – Hopes and Fears of the Querent.

Record card drawn and your interpretation of it:

Follow up, what actually occurred? Record how your interpretation of the card was accurate or inaccurate and why you think that happened:

Position 10 – The Ultimate Outcome of the matter at hand if the Querent maintains the same behaviors.

Record card drawn and your interpretation of it:

Follow up, what actually occurred? Record how your interpretation of the card was accurate or inaccurate and why you think that happened:

Summarize your thoughts on this Reading:

Reading Number: ______________________________Date of Reading: _______________

Question Asked:

____

____

Position 1 – The Significator, the influences surrounding the Querent at this time. What is on the Querent's mind or the influences surrounding the Querent at this time?

Record card drawn and your interpretation of it:

____

____

____

____

Follow up, what actually occurred? Record how your interpretation of the card was accurate or inaccurate and why you think that happened:

____

____

____

____

Position 2 – The Crossing Card, forces working for or against the Querent at this time.

Record card drawn and your interpretation of it:

____

____

____

____

Follow up, what actually occurred? Record how your interpretation of the card was accurate or inaccurate and why you think that happened:

Position 3 – The Crowning Card, the influence that is hanging over the entire situation at this time.

Record card drawn and your interpretation of it:

Follow up, what actually occurred? Record how your interpretation of the card was accurate or inaccurate and why you think that happened:

Position 4 – The Base of the Matter, already a part of the Querent's experience.

Record card drawn and your interpretation of it:

Follow up, what actually occurred? Record how your interpretation of the card was accurate or inaccurate and why you think that happened:

Position 5 – Present and Passing, the influences that are active in the Querent's life at this time, but are exiting at the time of the reading.

Record card drawn and your interpretation of it:

Follow up, what actually occurred? Record how your interpretation of the card was accurate or inaccurate and why you think that happened:

Position 6 – Immediate Future, what the Querent can expect within the next two to three weeks.

Record card drawn and your interpretation of it:

Follow up, what actually occurred? Record how your interpretation of the card was accurate or inaccurate and why you think that happened:

Position 7 – Near Future, what the Querent can expect within the next three weeks to two months if they maintain the current path.

Record card drawn and your interpretation of it:

Follow up, what actually occurred? Record how your interpretation of the card was accurate or inaccurate and why you think that happened:

Position 8 – How friends and family view the situation.

Record card drawn and your interpretation of it:

Follow up, what actually occurred? Record how your interpretation of the card was accurate or inaccurate and why you think that happened:

Position 9 – Hopes and Fears of the Querent.

Record card drawn and your interpretation of it:

Follow up, what actually occurred? Record how your interpretation of the card was accurate or inaccurate and why you think that happened:

Position 10 – The Ultimate Outcome of the matter at hand if the Querent maintains the same behaviors.

Record card drawn and your interpretation of it:

Follow up, what actually occurred? Record how your interpretation of the card was accurate or inaccurate and why you think that happened:

Summarize your thoughts on this Reading:

Reading Number: ______________________________Date of Reading: _______________

Question Asked:

____

____

Position 1 – The Significator, the influences surrounding the Querent at this time. What is on the Querent's mind or the influences surrounding the Querent at this time?

Record card drawn and your interpretation of it:

____

____

____

____

Follow up, what actually occurred? Record how your interpretation of the card was accurate or inaccurate and why you think that happened:

____

____

____

____

Position 2 – The Crossing Card, forces working for or against the Querent at this time.

Record card drawn and your interpretation of it:

____

____

____

____

Follow up, what actually occurred? Record how your interpretation of the card was accurate or inaccurate and why you think that happened:

Position 3 – The Crowning Card, the influence that is hanging over the entire situation at this time.

Record card drawn and your interpretation of it:

Follow up, what actually occurred? Record how your interpretation of the card was accurate or inaccurate and why you think that happened:

Position 4 – The Base of the Matter, already a part of the Querent's experience.

Record card drawn and your interpretation of it:

Follow up, what actually occurred? Record how your interpretation of the card was accurate or inaccurate and why you think that happened:

Position 5 – Present and Passing, the influences that are active in the Querent's life at this time, but are exiting at the time of the reading.

Record card drawn and your interpretation of it:

Follow up, what actually occurred? Record how your interpretation of the card was accurate or inaccurate and why you think that happened:

Position 6 – Immediate Future, what the Querent can expect within the next two to three weeks.

Record card drawn and your interpretation of it:

Follow up, what actually occurred? Record how your interpretation of the card was accurate or inaccurate and why you think that happened:

Position 7 – Near Future, what the Querent can expect within the next three weeks to two months if they maintain the current path.

Record card drawn and your interpretation of it:

Follow up, what actually occurred? Record how your interpretation of the card was accurate or inaccurate and why you think that happened:

Position 8 – How friends and family view the situation.

Record card drawn and your interpretation of it:

Follow up, what actually occurred? Record how your interpretation of the card was accurate or inaccurate and why you think that happened:

Position 9 – Hopes and Fears of the Querent.

Record card drawn and your interpretation of it:

Follow up, what actually occurred? Record how your interpretation of the card was accurate or inaccurate and why you think that happened:

Position 10 – The Ultimate Outcome of the matter at hand if the Querent maintains the same behaviors.

Record card drawn and your interpretation of it:

Follow up, what actually occurred? Record how your interpretation of the card was accurate or inaccurate and why you think that happened:

Summarize your thoughts on this Reading:

Reading Number: ______________________________Date of Reading: ______________

Question Asked:

____

____

Position 1 – The Significator, the influences surrounding the Querent at this time. What is on the Querent's mind or the influences surrounding the Querent at this time?

Record card drawn and your interpretation of it:

____

____

____

____

Follow up, what actually occurred? Record how your interpretation of the card was accurate or inaccurate and why you think that happened:

____

____

____

____

Position 2 – The Crossing Card, forces working for or against the Querent at this time.

Record card drawn and your interpretation of it:

____

____

____

____

Follow up, what actually occurred? Record how your interpretation of the card was accurate or inaccurate and why you think that happened:

Position 3 – The Crowning Card, the influence that is hanging over the entire situation at this time.

Record card drawn and your interpretation of it:

Follow up, what actually occurred? Record how your interpretation of the card was accurate or inaccurate and why you think that happened:

Position 4 – The Base of the Matter, already a part of the Querent's experience.

Record card drawn and your interpretation of it:

Follow up, what actually occurred? Record how your interpretation of the card was accurate or inaccurate and why you think that happened:

Position 5 – Present and Passing, the influences that are active in the Querent's life at this time, but are exiting at the time of the reading.

Record card drawn and your interpretation of it:

Follow up, what actually occurred? Record how your interpretation of the card was accurate or inaccurate and why you think that happened:

Position 6 – Immediate Future, what the Querent can expect within the next two to three weeks.

Record card drawn and your interpretation of it:

Follow up, what actually occurred? Record how your interpretation of the card was accurate or inaccurate and why you think that happened:

Position 7 – Near Future, what the Querent can expect within the next three weeks to two months if they maintain the current path.

Record card drawn and your interpretation of it:

Follow up, what actually occurred? Record how your interpretation of the card was accurate or inaccurate and why you think that happened:

Position 8 – How friends and family view the situation.

Record card drawn and your interpretation of it:

Follow up, what actually occurred? Record how your interpretation of the card was accurate or inaccurate and why you think that happened:

Position 9 – Hopes and Fears of the Querent.

Record card drawn and your interpretation of it:

Follow up, what actually occurred? Record how your interpretation of the card was accurate or inaccurate and why you think that happened:

Position 10 – The Ultimate Outcome of the matter at hand if the Querent maintains the same behaviors.

Record card drawn and your interpretation of it:

Follow up, what actually occurred? Record how your interpretation of the card was accurate or inaccurate and why you think that happened:

Summarize your thoughts on this Reading:

Reading Number: ______________________________ Date of Reading: ______________

Question Asked:

____

____

Position 1 – The Significator, the influences surrounding the Querent at this time. What is on the Querent's mind or the influences surrounding the Querent at this time?

Record card drawn and your interpretation of it:

____

____

____

____

Follow up, what actually occurred? Record how your interpretation of the card was accurate or inaccurate and why you think that happened:

____

____

____

____

Position 2 – The Crossing Card, forces working for or against the Querent at this time.

Record card drawn and your interpretation of it:

____

____

____

____

Follow up, what actually occurred? Record how your interpretation of the card was accurate or inaccurate and why you think that happened:

Position 3 – The Crowning Card, the influence that is hanging over the entire situation at this time.

Record card drawn and your interpretation of it:

Follow up, what actually occurred? Record how your interpretation of the card was accurate or inaccurate and why you think that happened:

Position 4 – The Base of the Matter, already a part of the Querent's experience.

Record card drawn and your interpretation of it:

Follow up, what actually occurred? Record how your interpretation of the card was accurate or inaccurate and why you think that happened:

Position 5 – Present and Passing, the influences that are active in the Querent's life at this time, but are exiting at the time of the reading.

Record card drawn and your interpretation of it:

Follow up, what actually occurred? Record how your interpretation of the card was accurate or inaccurate and why you think that happened:

Position 6 – Immediate Future, what the Querent can expect within the next two to three weeks.

Record card drawn and your interpretation of it:

Follow up, what actually occurred? Record how your interpretation of the card was accurate or inaccurate and why you think that happened:

Position 7 – Near Future, what the Querent can expect within the next three weeks to two months if they maintain the current path.

Record card drawn and your interpretation of it:

Follow up, what actually occurred? Record how your interpretation of the card was accurate or inaccurate and why you think that happened:

Position 8 – How friends and family view the situation.

Record card drawn and your interpretation of it:

Follow up, what actually occurred? Record how your interpretation of the card was accurate or inaccurate and why you think that happened:

Position 9 – Hopes and Fears of the Querent.

Record card drawn and your interpretation of it:

Follow up, what actually occurred? Record how your interpretation of the card was accurate or inaccurate and why you think that happened:

Position 10 – The Ultimate Outcome of the matter at hand if the Querent maintains the same behaviors.

Record card drawn and your interpretation of it:

Follow up, what actually occurred? Record how your interpretation of the card was accurate or inaccurate and why you think that happened:

Summarize your thoughts on this Reading:

Reading Number: ______________________________Date of Reading: _______________

Question Asked:

____

____

Position 1 – The Significator, the influences surrounding the Querent at this time. What is on the Querent's mind or the influences surrounding the Querent at this time?

Record card drawn and your interpretation of it:

____

____

____

____

Follow up, what actually occurred? Record how your interpretation of the card was accurate or inaccurate and why you think that happened:

____

____

____

____

Position 2 – The Crossing Card, forces working for or against the Querent at this time.

Record card drawn and your interpretation of it:

____

____

____

____

Follow up, what actually occurred? Record how your interpretation of the card was accurate or inaccurate and why you think that happened:

Position 3 – The Crowning Card, the influence that is hanging over the entire situation at this time.

Record card drawn and your interpretation of it:

Follow up, what actually occurred? Record how your interpretation of the card was accurate or inaccurate and why you think that happened:

Position 4 – The Base of the Matter, already a part of the Querent's experience.

Record card drawn and your interpretation of it:

Follow up, what actually occurred? Record how your interpretation of the card was accurate or inaccurate and why you think that happened:

Position 5 – Present and Passing, the influences that are active in the Querent's life at this time, but are exiting at the time of the reading.

Record card drawn and your interpretation of it:

Follow up, what actually occurred? Record how your interpretation of the card was accurate or inaccurate and why you think that happened:

Position 6 – Immediate Future, what the Querent can expect within the next two to three weeks.

Record card drawn and your interpretation of it:

Follow up, what actually occurred? Record how your interpretation of the card was accurate or inaccurate and why you think that happened:

Position 7 – Near Future, what the Querent can expect within the next three weeks to two months if they maintain the current path.

Record card drawn and your interpretation of it:

Follow up, what actually occurred? Record how your interpretation of the card was accurate or inaccurate and why you think that happened:

Position 8 – How friends and family view the situation.

Record card drawn and your interpretation of it:

Follow up, what actually occurred? Record how your interpretation of the card was accurate or inaccurate and why you think that happened:

Position 9 – Hopes and Fears of the Querent.

Record card drawn and your interpretation of it:

Follow up, what actually occurred? Record how your interpretation of the card was accurate or inaccurate and why you think that happened:

Position 10 – The Ultimate Outcome of the matter at hand if the Querent maintains the same behaviors.

Record card drawn and your interpretation of it:

Follow up, what actually occurred? Record how your interpretation of the card was accurate or inaccurate and why you think that happened:

Summarize your thoughts on this Reading:

Reading Number: ______________________________ Date of Reading: ______________

Question Asked:

____

____

Position 1 – The Significator, the influences surrounding the Querent at this time. What is on the Querent's mind or the influences surrounding the Querent at this time?

Record card drawn and your interpretation of it:

____

____

____

____

Follow up, what actually occurred? Record how your interpretation of the card was accurate or inaccurate and why you think that happened:

____

____

____

____

Position 2 – The Crossing Card, forces working for or against the Querent at this time.

Record card drawn and your interpretation of it:

____

____

____

____

____

Follow up, what actually occurred? Record how your interpretation of the card was accurate or inaccurate and why you think that happened:

Position 3 – The Crowning Card, the influence that is hanging over the entire situation at this time.

Record card drawn and your interpretation of it:

Follow up, what actually occurred? Record how your interpretation of the card was accurate or inaccurate and why you think that happened:

Position 4 – The Base of the Matter, already a part of the Querent's experience.

Record card drawn and your interpretation of it:

Follow up, what actually occurred? Record how your interpretation of the card was accurate or inaccurate and why you think that happened:

Position 5 – Present and Passing, the influences that are active in the Querent's life at this time, but are exiting at the time of the reading.

Record card drawn and your interpretation of it:

Follow up, what actually occurred? Record how your interpretation of the card was accurate or inaccurate and why you think that happened:

Position 6 – Immediate Future, what the Querent can expect within the next two to three weeks.

Record card drawn and your interpretation of it:

Follow up, what actually occurred? Record how your interpretation of the card was accurate or inaccurate and why you think that happened:

Position 7 – Near Future, what the Querent can expect within the next three weeks to two months if they maintain the current path.

Record card drawn and your interpretation of it:

Follow up, what actually occurred? Record how your interpretation of the card was accurate or inaccurate and why you think that happened:

Position 8 – How friends and family view the situation.

Record card drawn and your interpretation of it:

Follow up, what actually occurred? Record how your interpretation of the card was accurate or inaccurate and why you think that happened:

Position 9 – Hopes and Fears of the Querent.

Record card drawn and your interpretation of it:

Follow up, what actually occurred? Record how your interpretation of the card was accurate or inaccurate and why you think that happened:

Position 10 – The Ultimate Outcome of the matter at hand if the Querent maintains the same behaviors.

Record card drawn and your interpretation of it:

Follow up, what actually occurred? Record how your interpretation of the card was accurate or inaccurate and why you think that happened:

Summarize your thoughts on this Reading:

Reading Number: ______________________________ Date of Reading: ______________

Question Asked:

____

____

Position 1 – The Significator, the influences surrounding the Querent at this time. What is on the Querent's mind or the influences surrounding the Querent at this time?

Record card drawn and your interpretation of it:

____

____

____

____

Follow up, what actually occurred? Record how your interpretation of the card was accurate or inaccurate and why you think that happened:

____

____

____

____

Position 2 – The Crossing Card, forces working for or against the Querent at this time.

Record card drawn and your interpretation of it:

____

____

____

____

____

Follow up, what actually occurred? Record how your interpretation of the card was accurate or inaccurate and why you think that happened:

Position 3 – The Crowning Card, the influence that is hanging over the entire situation at this time.

Record card drawn and your interpretation of it:

Follow up, what actually occurred? Record how your interpretation of the card was accurate or inaccurate and why you think that happened:

Position 4 – The Base of the Matter, already a part of the Querent's experience.

Record card drawn and your interpretation of it:

Follow up, what actually occurred? Record how your interpretation of the card was accurate or inaccurate and why you think that happened:

Position 5 – Present and Passing, the influences that are active in the Querent's life at this time, but are exiting at the time of the reading.

Record card drawn and your interpretation of it:

Follow up, what actually occurred? Record how your interpretation of the card was accurate or inaccurate and why you think that happened:

Position 6 – Immediate Future, what the Querent can expect within the next two to three weeks.

Record card drawn and your interpretation of it:

Follow up, what actually occurred? Record how your interpretation of the card was accurate or inaccurate and why you think that happened:

Position 7 – Near Future, what the Querent can expect within the next three weeks to two months if they maintain the current path.

Record card drawn and your interpretation of it:

Follow up, what actually occurred? Record how your interpretation of the card was accurate or inaccurate and why you think that happened:

Position 8 – How friends and family view the situation.

Record card drawn and your interpretation of it:

Follow up, what actually occurred? Record how your interpretation of the card was accurate or inaccurate and why you think that happened:

Position 9 – Hopes and Fears of the Querent.

Record card drawn and your interpretation of it:

Follow up, what actually occurred? Record how your interpretation of the card was accurate or inaccurate and why you think that happened:

Position 10 – The Ultimate Outcome of the matter at hand if the Querent maintains the same behaviors.

Record card drawn and your interpretation of it:

Follow up, what actually occurred? Record how your interpretation of the card was accurate or inaccurate and why you think that happened:

Summarize your thoughts on this Reading:

Reading Number: ______________________________Date of Reading: ______________

Question Asked:

____

____

Position 1 – The Significator, the influences surrounding the Querent at this time. What is on the Querent's mind or the influences surrounding the Querent at this time?

Record card drawn and your interpretation of it:

____

____

____

____

Follow up, what actually occurred? Record how your interpretation of the card was accurate or inaccurate and why you think that happened:

____

____

____

____

Position 2 – The Crossing Card, forces working for or against the Querent at this time.

Record card drawn and your interpretation of it:

____

____

____

____

____

Follow up, what actually occurred? Record how your interpretation of the card was accurate or inaccurate and why you think that happened:

Position 3 – The Crowning Card, the influence that is hanging over the entire situation at this time.

Record card drawn and your interpretation of it:

Follow up, what actually occurred? Record how your interpretation of the card was accurate or inaccurate and why you think that happened:

Position 4 – The Base of the Matter, already a part of the Querent's experience.

Record card drawn and your interpretation of it:

Follow up, what actually occurred? Record how your interpretation of the card was accurate or inaccurate and why you think that happened:

Position 5 – Present and Passing, the influences that are active in the Querent's life at this time, but are exiting at the time of the reading.

Record card drawn and your interpretation of it:

Follow up, what actually occurred? Record how your interpretation of the card was accurate or inaccurate and why you think that happened:

Position 6 – Immediate Future, what the Querent can expect within the next two to three weeks.

Record card drawn and your interpretation of it:

Follow up, what actually occurred? Record how your interpretation of the card was accurate or inaccurate and why you think that happened:

Position 7 – Near Future, what the Querent can expect within the next three weeks to two months if they maintain the current path.

Record card drawn and your interpretation of it:

Follow up, what actually occurred? Record how your interpretation of the card was accurate or inaccurate and why you think that happened:

Position 8 – How friends and family view the situation.

Record card drawn and your interpretation of it:

Follow up, what actually occurred? Record how your interpretation of the card was accurate or inaccurate and why you think that happened:

Position 9 – Hopes and Fears of the Querent.

Record card drawn and your interpretation of it:

Follow up, what actually occurred? Record how your interpretation of the card was accurate or inaccurate and why you think that happened:

Position 10 – The Ultimate Outcome of the matter at hand if the Querent maintains the same behaviors.

Record card drawn and your interpretation of it:

Follow up, what actually occurred? Record how your interpretation of the card was accurate or inaccurate and why you think that happened:

Summarize your thoughts on this Reading:

Reading Number: ______________________________ Date of Reading: ______________

Question Asked:

____

____

Position 1 – The Significator, the influences surrounding the Querent at this time. What is on the Querent's mind or the influences surrounding the Querent at this time?

Record card drawn and your interpretation of it:

____

____

____

____

Follow up, what actually occurred? Record how your interpretation of the card was accurate or inaccurate and why you think that happened:

____

____

____

____

Position 2 – The Crossing Card, forces working for or against the Querent at this time.

Record card drawn and your interpretation of it:

____

____

____

____

Follow up, what actually occurred? Record how your interpretation of the card was accurate or inaccurate and why you think that happened:

Position 3 – The Crowning Card, the influence that is hanging over the entire situation at this time.

Record card drawn and your interpretation of it:

Follow up, what actually occurred? Record how your interpretation of the card was accurate or inaccurate and why you think that happened:

Position 4 – The Base of the Matter, already a part of the Querent's experience.

Record card drawn and your interpretation of it:

Follow up, what actually occurred? Record how your interpretation of the card was accurate or inaccurate and why you think that happened:

Position 5 – Present and Passing, the influences that are active in the Querent's life at this time, but are exiting at the time of the reading.

Record card drawn and your interpretation of it:

Follow up, what actually occurred? Record how your interpretation of the card was accurate or inaccurate and why you think that happened:

Position 6 – Immediate Future, what the Querent can expect within the next two to three weeks.

Record card drawn and your interpretation of it:

Follow up, what actually occurred? Record how your interpretation of the card was accurate or inaccurate and why you think that happened:

Position 7 – Near Future, what the Querent can expect within the next three weeks to two months if they maintain the current path.

Record card drawn and your interpretation of it:

Follow up, what actually occurred? Record how your interpretation of the card was accurate or inaccurate and why you think that happened:

Position 8 – How friends and family view the situation.

Record card drawn and your interpretation of it:

Follow up, what actually occurred? Record how your interpretation of the card was accurate or inaccurate and why you think that happened:

Position 9 – Hopes and Fears of the Querent.

Record card drawn and your interpretation of it:

Follow up, what actually occurred? Record how your interpretation of the card was accurate or inaccurate and why you think that happened:

Position 10 – The Ultimate Outcome of the matter at hand if the Querent maintains the same behaviors.

Record card drawn and your interpretation of it:

Follow up, what actually occurred? Record how your interpretation of the card was accurate or inaccurate and why you think that happened:

Summarize your thoughts on this Reading:

Reading Number: ______________________________ Date of Reading: ______________

Question Asked:

____

____

Position 1 – The Significator, the influences surrounding the Querent at this time. What is on the Querent's mind or the influences surrounding the Querent at this time?

Record card drawn and your interpretation of it:

____

____

____

____

Follow up, what actually occurred? Record how your interpretation of the card was accurate or inaccurate and why you think that happened:

____

____

____

____

Position 2 – The Crossing Card, forces working for or against the Querent at this time.

Record card drawn and your interpretation of it:

____

____

____

____

Follow up, what actually occurred? Record how your interpretation of the card was accurate or inaccurate and why you think that happened:

Position 3 – The Crowning Card, the influence that is hanging over the entire situation at this time.

Record card drawn and your interpretation of it:

Follow up, what actually occurred? Record how your interpretation of the card was accurate or inaccurate and why you think that happened:

Position 4 – The Base of the Matter, already a part of the Querent's experience.

Record card drawn and your interpretation of it:

Follow up, what actually occurred? Record how your interpretation of the card was accurate or inaccurate and why you think that happened:

Position 5 – Present and Passing, the influences that are active in the Querent's life at this time, but are exiting at the time of the reading.

Record card drawn and your interpretation of it:

Follow up, what actually occurred? Record how your interpretation of the card was accurate or inaccurate and why you think that happened:

Position 6 – Immediate Future, what the Querent can expect within the next two to three weeks.

Record card drawn and your interpretation of it:

Follow up, what actually occurred? Record how your interpretation of the card was accurate or inaccurate and why you think that happened:

Position 7 – Near Future, what the Querent can expect within the next three weeks to two months if they maintain the current path.

Record card drawn and your interpretation of it:

Follow up, what actually occurred? Record how your interpretation of the card was accurate or inaccurate and why you think that happened:

Position 8 – How friends and family view the situation.

Record card drawn and your interpretation of it:

Follow up, what actually occurred? Record how your interpretation of the card was accurate or inaccurate and why you think that happened:

Position 9 – Hopes and Fears of the Querent.

Record card drawn and your interpretation of it:

Follow up, what actually occurred? Record how your interpretation of the card was accurate or inaccurate and why you think that happened:

Position 10 – The Ultimate Outcome of the matter at hand if the Querent maintains the same behaviors.

Record card drawn and your interpretation of it:

Follow up, what actually occurred? Record how your interpretation of the card was accurate or inaccurate and why you think that happened:

Summarize your thoughts on this Reading:

Reading Number: ______________________________Date of Reading: ______________

Question Asked:

____

____

Position 1 – The Significator, the influences surrounding the Querent at this time. What is on the Querent's mind or the influences surrounding the Querent at this time?

Record card drawn and your interpretation of it:

____

____

____

____

Follow up, what actually occurred? Record how your interpretation of the card was accurate or inaccurate and why you think that happened:

____

____

____

____

Position 2 – The Crossing Card, forces working for or against the Querent at this time.

Record card drawn and your interpretation of it:

____

____

____

____

____

Follow up, what actually occurred? Record how your interpretation of the card was accurate or inaccurate and why you think that happened:

Position 3 – The Crowning Card, the influence that is hanging over the entire situation at this time.

Record card drawn and your interpretation of it:

Follow up, what actually occurred? Record how your interpretation of the card was accurate or inaccurate and why you think that happened:

Position 4 – The Base of the Matter, already a part of the Querent's experience.

Record card drawn and your interpretation of it:

Follow up, what actually occurred? Record how your interpretation of the card was accurate or inaccurate and why you think that happened:

Position 5 – Present and Passing, the influences that are active in the Querent's life at this time, but are exiting at the time of the reading.

Record card drawn and your interpretation of it:

Follow up, what actually occurred? Record how your interpretation of the card was accurate or inaccurate and why you think that happened:

Position 6 – Immediate Future, what the Querent can expect within the next two to three weeks.

Record card drawn and your interpretation of it:

Follow up, what actually occurred? Record how your interpretation of the card was accurate or inaccurate and why you think that happened:

Position 7 – Near Future, what the Querent can expect within the next three weeks to two months if they maintain the current path.

Record card drawn and your interpretation of it:

Follow up, what actually occurred? Record how your interpretation of the card was accurate or inaccurate and why you think that happened:

Position 8 – How friends and family view the situation.

Record card drawn and your interpretation of it:

Follow up, what actually occurred? Record how your interpretation of the card was accurate or inaccurate and why you think that happened:

Position 9 – Hopes and Fears of the Querent.

Record card drawn and your interpretation of it:

Follow up, what actually occurred? Record how your interpretation of the card was accurate or inaccurate and why you think that happened:

Position 10 – The Ultimate Outcome of the matter at hand if the Querent maintains the same behaviors.

Record card drawn and your interpretation of it:

Follow up, what actually occurred? Record how your interpretation of the card was accurate or inaccurate and why you think that happened:

Summarize your thoughts on this Reading:

Reading Number: ______________________________ Date of Reading: ______________

Question Asked:

____

____

Position 1 – The Significator, the influences surrounding the Querent at this time. What is on the Querent's mind or the influences surrounding the Querent at this time?

Record card drawn and your interpretation of it:

____

____

____

____

Follow up, what actually occurred? Record how your interpretation of the card was accurate or inaccurate and why you think that happened:

____

____

____

____

Position 2 – The Crossing Card, forces working for or against the Querent at this time.

Record card drawn and your interpretation of it:

____

____

____

____

Follow up, what actually occurred? Record how your interpretation of the card was accurate or inaccurate and why you think that happened:

Position 3 – The Crowning Card, the influence that is hanging over the entire situation at this time.

Record card drawn and your interpretation of it:

Follow up, what actually occurred? Record how your interpretation of the card was accurate or inaccurate and why you think that happened:

Position 4 – The Base of the Matter, already a part of the Querent's experience.

Record card drawn and your interpretation of it:

Follow up, what actually occurred? Record how your interpretation of the card was accurate or inaccurate and why you think that happened:

Position 5 – Present and Passing, the influences that are active in the Querent's life at this time, but are exiting at the time of the reading.

Record card drawn and your interpretation of it:

Follow up, what actually occurred? Record how your interpretation of the card was accurate or inaccurate and why you think that happened:

Position 6 – Immediate Future, what the Querent can expect within the next two to three weeks.

Record card drawn and your interpretation of it:

Follow up, what actually occurred? Record how your interpretation of the card was accurate or inaccurate and why you think that happened:

Position 7 – Near Future, what the Querent can expect within the next three weeks to two months if they maintain the current path.

Record card drawn and your interpretation of it:

Follow up, what actually occurred? Record how your interpretation of the card was accurate or inaccurate and why you think that happened:

Position 8 – How friends and family view the situation.

Record card drawn and your interpretation of it:

Follow up, what actually occurred? Record how your interpretation of the card was accurate or inaccurate and why you think that happened:

Position 9 – Hopes and Fears of the Querent.

Record card drawn and your interpretation of it:

Follow up, what actually occurred? Record how your interpretation of the card was accurate or inaccurate and why you think that happened:

Position 10 – The Ultimate Outcome of the matter at hand if the Querent maintains the same behaviors.

Record card drawn and your interpretation of it:

Follow up, what actually occurred? Record how your interpretation of the card was accurate or inaccurate and why you think that happened:

Summarize your thoughts on this Reading:

Reading Number: ______________________________ Date of Reading: _______________

Question Asked:

____

____

Position 1 – The Significator, the influences surrounding the Querent at this time. What is on the Querent's mind or the influences surrounding the Querent at this time?

Record card drawn and your interpretation of it:

____

____

____

____

Follow up, what actually occurred? Record how your interpretation of the card was accurate or inaccurate and why you think that happened:

____

____

____

____

Position 2 – The Crossing Card, forces working for or against the Querent at this time.

Record card drawn and your interpretation of it:

____

____

____

____

Follow up, what actually occurred? Record how your interpretation of the card was accurate or inaccurate and why you think that happened:

Position 3 – The Crowning Card, the influence that is hanging over the entire situation at this time.

Record card drawn and your interpretation of it:

Follow up, what actually occurred? Record how your interpretation of the card was accurate or inaccurate and why you think that happened:

Position 4 – The Base of the Matter, already a part of the Querent's experience.

Record card drawn and your interpretation of it:

Follow up, what actually occurred? Record how your interpretation of the card was accurate or inaccurate and why you think that happened:

Position 5 – Present and Passing, the influences that are active in the Querent's life at this time, but are exiting at the time of the reading.

Record card drawn and your interpretation of it:

Follow up, what actually occurred? Record how your interpretation of the card was accurate or inaccurate and why you think that happened:

Position 6 – Immediate Future, what the Querent can expect within the next two to three weeks.

Record card drawn and your interpretation of it:

Follow up, what actually occurred? Record how your interpretation of the card was accurate or inaccurate and why you think that happened:

Position 7 – Near Future, what the Querent can expect within the next three weeks to two months if they maintain the current path.

Record card drawn and your interpretation of it:

Follow up, what actually occurred? Record how your interpretation of the card was accurate or inaccurate and why you think that happened:

Position 8 – How friends and family view the situation.

Record card drawn and your interpretation of it:

Follow up, what actually occurred? Record how your interpretation of the card was accurate or inaccurate and why you think that happened:

Position 9 – Hopes and Fears of the Querent.

Record card drawn and your interpretation of it:

Follow up, what actually occurred? Record how your interpretation of the card was accurate or inaccurate and why you think that happened:

Position 10 – The Ultimate Outcome of the matter at hand if the Querent maintains the same behaviors.

Record card drawn and your interpretation of it:

Follow up, what actually occurred? Record how your interpretation of the card was accurate or inaccurate and why you think that happened:

Summarize your thoughts on this Reading:

13464700R00140

Printed in Great Britain
by Amazon.co.uk, Ltd.,
Marston Gate.